Blood and Candles

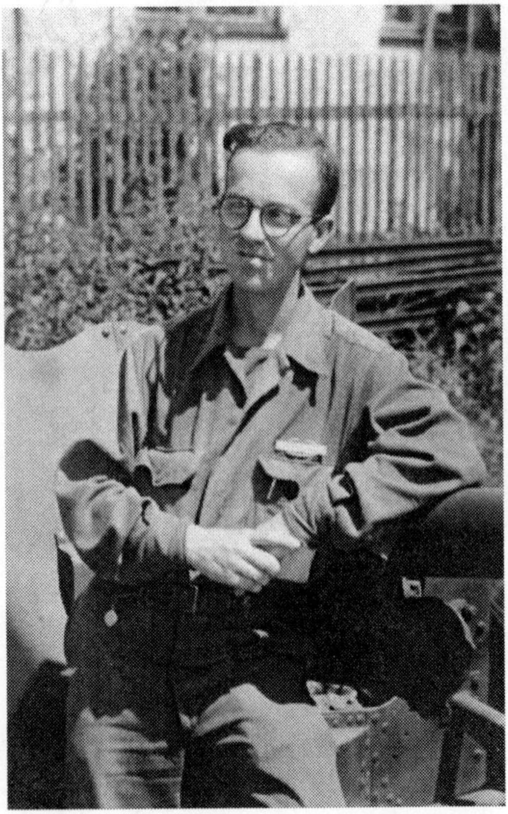

Blood and Candles

The Story of a World War II Infantryman

Edward T. Richardson, Jr.

Trafford Press

© 2002 by Edward T. Richardson, Jr. All rights reserved.

Book design and typography by Bruce Kennett Studio.

No part of this publication may be reproduced, stored in a retrieval system, or transmitted, in any form or by any means, electronic, mechanical, photocopying, recording, or otherwise, without the written prior permission of the author.

FRONTISPIECE The author at Wolnzach, Bavaria, June 1945, leaning on an anti-tank gun kept in place after the end of the War because of rumors that the SS and Hitler Youth were hiding in the mountains and planning a surprise attack.

ON THE COVER The headquarters staff of Company B, 60th Infantry Regiment of the 9th Infantry Division. The author is sitting on the jeep bumper at the right. Captain K, the company commander, is standing at the left. This photo was taken in the Hartz Mountains during a sweep to flush out groups of SS and Hitler Youth who were fighting guerrilla style, even after it became apparent that the War was nearly over. Many of the regular German Army troops had already surrendered to the Americans to avoid having to surrender to the Russians.

National Library of Canada Cataloguing in Publication

Richardson, Edward T., 1921-
    Blood and candles : the story of a World War II infantryman / Edward T. Richardson.

ISBN 1-55369-297-7
    1. Richardson, Edward T., 1921-. 2. World War, 1939-1945—Personal narratives, American. 3. United States. Army—Biography. 4. Soldiers—United States—Biography. I. Title.

D811.R52 2002   940.54'8173   C2002-901174-4

TRAFFORD

This book was published *on-demand* in cooperation with Trafford Publishing. On-demand publishing is a unique process and service of making a book available for retail sale to the public taking advantage of on-demand manufacturing and Internet marketing. **On-demand publishing** includes promotions, retail sales, manufacturing, order fulfilment, accounting and collecting royalties on behalf of the author.

Suite 6E, 2333 Government St., Victoria, B.C. V8T 4P4, CANADA
Phone   250-383-6864   Toll-free   1-888-232-4444 (Canada & US)
Fax   250-383-6804   E-mail   sales@trafford.com
Web site www.trafford.com   TRAFFORD PUBLISHING IS A DIVISION OF TRAFFORD HOLDINGS LTD.
Trafford Catalogue #02-0110   www.trafford.com/robots/02-0110.html

10   9   8   7   6   5   4   3   2   1

Contents

List of Illustrations	vii
Preface	ix
I Basic Training	1
II Special Training	13
III Basic All Over Again	18
IV To Combat	23
V To the Roer	37
VI The Battle of the Bulge	48
VII On to the Rhine	54
VIII The Final Push	73
IX VE Day in Paris	91
X Summer in Paris	110
XI Occupation Duty	123
XII Heading Home	134
Postscript	137
About the Author	138

Illustrations

The author at Wolznach	Frontispiece
The author on a hill above Remagen	68
Company B Headquarters Staff	76
At Bitterfeld, just before VE Day	82
Announcement of the War's end, Soissons	90
The view from Berchtesgaden	101
Eagle's Nest, exterior	102
Eagle's Nest, interior	103
The author at Eagle's Nest	104
Ruins of an arch, Munich	106
The great poet Schiller	107
Fallen statues, Munich	108
University of Munich	109
View from the author's lodgings, Paris	113
The batallion kitchen crew	132

*Dedicated to Charlton Smith,
who encouraged me to tell the story of
my experiences as a soldier in World War II,
and who provided invaluable assistance
in the publication of this book.*

Preface

This book began as a spoken narration onto tape. It has been transcribed into written form essentially as I dictated it. In telling this story I wanted to get beyond the account of victory in battle. While that is the logical climax to such a narration, I wanted to go deeper. What did we soldiers do between battles, which, after all, occupied only the smaller part of our time at the front? What did we see, and what did we think about what we saw? How did many among us die? How did we change under the daily stress? In short, what was life really like in World War II, in combat with Nazi Germany in her death throes?

My military career extended through a period just short of three years. I went from college directly into the Army, underwent special training, but went into and survived over seven months of infantry combat, the last months of the War in Europe. I enjoyed incredible good luck in escaping injury, being only one of about three of the sixty or more original members of my platoon who were not killed or seriously wounded in combat. I was also very fortunate to be in Paris on VE Day, and to be able to spend the first summer after the War in Europe, in Paris, later serving in the Army of Occupation.

I went on active duty on the first day of July 1943, and was discharged in March 1946. Between those dates I experienced the frightening, the pathetic, the moving, the ridiculous, the funny and the unbelievable, all to a degree I would not have thought possible. By means of this book I would like to share those experiences with others.

Just short of my twenty-second birthday I entered the Army a bookish, somewhat introverted person. For what happened then, read on.

Blood and Candles

1

Basic Training

The beginning of my Army experience was the induction examination here in South Portland. We were lined up naked and passed through the examination one by one going through the VD scrutiny and the psychological exam – "Do you like girls?" There was a group from the Navy there picking out likely specimens suggesting they volunteer for the Navy, thereby escaping the draft which had got the rest of us. I was not among those chosen, not being a likely specimen I guess. At five foot five and 125 pounds, I had never been an athlete, although I did a lot of walking and bicycling. So I passed on into the regular Army category.

By the summer of 1943 the Army had gotten pretty hungry for recruits. There was a shortage of personnel in some departments. By that time I was determined to get into the Army. Although I dreaded it I felt it a duty. In 1943 we were deep in the War and things did not look very good at that time. My father had been in the Navy in World War I. A great-grandfather had been wounded in the Civil War and an ancestor had fought in the American Revolution. So I felt I had a duty to carry on that tradition. I had no idea what I was getting into. I was duly admitted and on the first day of July 1943 I went over to Union Station in Portland, Maine where trainloads and busloads of men were being brought in to take the train to Fort Devens.

There were two trains lined up side-by-side, one for the Navy and one for the Army. I stood to one side watching what appeared to be a good deal of confusion. I was also suffering from a bad headache. An Army sergeant stepped up to me, looked me over and said, "Well fella, you look as if you might be able to read and write." I said, "Well, I think so," and he handed me a file saying, "Here take this." He then put a band around my left arm on which were corporal stripes and said, "You are an acting corporal and you're charged with getting this gang of men to Fort Devens. Don't lose any of 'em and if any of 'em get disruptive, get tough with 'em." He then looked at me and grinned because of my small size. Most of these guys were from inland Maine. They were woodsmen, farmers, fishermen, and truck drivers. Any one of them could have tossed me over his shoulder and lugged me off without any problem.

The train left. We arrived at Fort Devens. I handed in my list. I'd not even bothered to try to take a count on the train because people were milling around so. At that point it was discovered that I had lost a man. The officer in charge gave me a bawling out, but then passed on and the missing man turned up two or three days later. He'd gotten on the Navy train instead of the Army. After a few days at Fort Devens doing mostly KP and cleanup work, I was shipped out along with another group to Camp Croft in South Carolina. Camp Croft was a new camp. It had been built just a couple of years before World War II. We were divided up into platoons and went about drilling and the other things necessary for basic training, one of which was practice in digging foxholes. The officer told us to choose up sides in pairs for this purpose. Two of us were not chosen, an older fellow and I. We had stood aside from the group somewhat. He was a thickset, short, dark man with a mustache and he appeared to be considerably older than the rest of us who were all either in our late teens or early twenties. I stepped up to him and said, "I guess we are a pair." He said, "It looks that way." We were assigned to our spot, given shovels and we started to dig. We had a time limit when the inspectors would come around and see what we'd done.

After the initial digging, my partner said to me, "Look, you stand aside and let me do the digging and you just bank up the soil I dig out around the edges." I agreed, not being much of a digger. Then I watched him and I have never seen a man dig so fast, so well and do such a good job as he did. A foxhole is supposed to be four feet deep, six feet long and four feet wide, or thereabouts, and he had it done before any of the other pairs were anywhere near finished and well before the deadline. The inspecting officer came around and we stood at attention by our hole. Many of the groups had not finished at all. We were praised and given the first award, which was largely the praise.

We then were given a break and I asked my partner, "What do you do in civilian life to become such a master of digging?" It turned out that he was a coal miner and he asked me what I did. I said, "I have been a student all my life up to this point." "Well good", he replied, "You must be able to read and write then," and I said, "Yes I can." Then he confessed to me that he needed help because he could neither read nor write, except his own name and one or two elementary words. He said he had been in the mines since he was in his middle teens and that his wife did all the reading and writing for them. She had instructed him that as soon as he got settled down in camp to find another soldier who could help him because she wrote him frequently. I told him I'd be glad to help and I wrote his letters for him the rest of the time we were at Camp Croft. I got quite familiar with his wife's letters and their respective points of view and was able to write his letters back to her as well as read her letters to him. It worked out very well.

Another ability arose from his experience in the coal mines. We were getting a hand grenade drill and the sergeant pulled an old trick, but none of us I guess were familiar with it. He was instructing us in the operation of a hand grenade and how to throw it and he fumbled one and dropped it on the ground. The pin had been pulled and it began to fizzle and we all jumped away as best we could and threw ourselves on the ground, except for my miner friend. With amazing swiftness, he grabbed the grenade and threw it. Of course it didn't explode. It had no explosive charge in it. It was simply the primer that had burnt and the sergeant had done that to see what our reaction would be. My friend did so well at this sort of thing that later they made him an acting sergeant for the drilling procedures.

This was just part of some fast learning that I underwent at the beginning of my training. I had never associated with any sort of people other than the sort that I was – an average, middle class, white person and more particularly, the type that would become a student, go to college and so on. Of course that military group was made up of the most diverse fellows with all kinds of backgrounds. Most of them were on the low end of the economic scale as well as the low end of the educational scale. I set out to get to know as many of them as I could and soon developed friendly relations with most all of them. That miner jolted me into awareness that a person with a college education could be completely inadequate in some environments, whereas an illiterate miner could be a lifesaver.

There were other people in that group that I became very friendly with. One was a mountain boy from Tennessee. He was a very good soldier as were many of those fellows from the southern Appalachians. I think they had it better in the Army than they'd ever had it at home and they'd had a gun in their hands ever since they could walk. This boy from Tennessee and I got on very well. One day he said to me, "Gee, Richie, you talk funny." There was also a boy from New York. He was eighteen years old and he had been a runner for a local cell of the Communist Party in New York, was a confirmed communist and immediately set out trying to convert his fellow soldiers. I had never met anyone who professed to be a communist before and so I started engaging him in conversations to try to figure out just what he had in mind and what was his rationale. I quickly found that he'd been completely brainwashed and all I could get out of him were canned statements of policy and that he himself was apparently rather stupid.

I began to feel sorry for the boy because guys began to shun him and mock him, and then I discovered that a little group of friends headed by this Tennessee boy that I knew were planning to get him into the woods on a Saturday night and rough him up rather badly. I confronted my friend and said, "Look, you can't do this. This is wrong. He has a right to his opinions even though we don't agree with him." I gave him the whole liberal argument and finally he and the others were convinced enough to agree that all they'd do would be to scare him. So they did that and they scared him very badly. I am not sure how they did it – threats, I guess, of what would happen to him. That got him hysterical and he ran to the company commander. The company commander formed the impression that he had something wrong with him emotionally and he sent him to the medics. The upshot of it was, although he came back for a short while, he was discharged under a medical discharge. That's the last we saw of him.

Then came a new lieutenant, Lieutenant Williams I think his name was. He took a dislike to me right from the start and it was mutual because it was one of those personality things. He took every opportunity he could to be deprecatory toward me in anything I did. I think he was particularly jealous because I was the only college graduate in the group, including him, who had been, I understood, a clerk in a department store in the women's goods department before he got his commission and had attended officers' training school. We didn't get on well at all and it first came out publicly when one of our orientation hours came up. At least once a week we had an orientation hour that consisted of one of the troops reading a printed bulletin that contained the Army's latest report of operations. Some of it was rather obviously propaganda to encourage us. They were full of foreign names, of course, and a large number of the fellows in the group had trouble enough reading ordinary text. They were completely lost trying to read one of those reports and the lieutenant was not much better at it than they were. Then he got an idea. He said very sarcastically one day, "Of course I realize everyone is having trouble with these foreign names and so on, but we have with us a college graduate. Private Richardson is a college graduate and I'm sure he would have no trouble with this." He said this with a sneer. I got up and read it through perfectly, knowing that I'd probably get in trouble as a result, and I did. He said, "Well, Private Richardson did so well he can read all of them." So I ended up with an extra job for a while.

Most of our hikes were at night because South Carolina in the summer is terribly hot and humid in the daytime and though the humidity hangs on at night, it cools off somewhat. Once we had a day hike of ten miles or so and it was early on and I hadn't gotten conditioned to the heat very well yet. Part way through I began to get dizzy and I fell out of formation. The lieutenant ordered me back in line and to keep on going, which I did for a while, but then I began to get dizzier and got nauseated with all the symptoms of heat exhaustion and sweating. I fell out again, on my hands and knees this time, and I was very dizzy and then gagging so the lieutenant said, "Well, if Private Richardson prefers to march on his hands and knees, he can do that." He ordered the corporal to accompany me and said to me, "You will crawl back to the camp on your hands and knees." There was about a half mile left. I was determined not to let him get the best of me, and I did crawl back to camp on my hands and knees, but that didn't finish it. When I got back he ordered me to spend the evening cleaning rifles, and for every little infraction for which he felt me guilty I was sent to the kitchen for KP duty.

We had an old-line mess sergeant. He had originally joined the Marines. When he got through with them he joined the Navy. When he got through with them he joined the Army and he was near retirement age. He was a very well-fed fellow and had rather an ugly disposition toward the troops generally. He finally took notice of the fact that I was showing up on KP with great frequency. He said, "What's with you soldier? You're over here two or three times a week. When do you get any drill? You must be a god-awful fuckup to be over here so much." I said, "Well, maybe I am, but the lieutenant doesn't like me and I don't like him very much." He said, "Oh, well, Lieutenant Williams, nobody likes that son of a bitch." So we began to get a little friendly and then I learned something about camp politics. It seems that we had home style dining. Each company was responsible for its own mess hall. Each round of troops going through led to a judgment of the excellence, or lack of it, of the mess hall and a pennant was given to the best one. If a mess hall got three pennants in succession, they got to keep one. We had received two pennants in succession and our mess sergeant was determined to keep the pennant this time. We were worked very rigorously keeping our place clean. In fact, they had to call off scrubbing the floors because we scrubbed them so much that the boards began to warp. At any rate, he said to me one day, "Private, you can help me a little bit." And I said, "What is it, Sergeant?" He said, "There's going to be an inspection this afternoon and, when normally you would be taking a break, I want you to be in here scrubbing on one of the tables. I will make it good with you later."

He had a spy in headquarters who let him know when the inspection was going to take place, so he knew when to have everything hunky-dory. In due course, about mid afternoon when it was terribly hot, an aging major showed up from headquarters to inspect. The mess sergeant had his new uniform on all pressed and neat. The major remarked how hot it was and mopped his brow. The mess sergeant said, "Would the major like a cool drink?" The major allowed, "Sergeant, that would be very nice." "And would the major like a little of the fruit salad that is going to be served to the troops tonight?" The major said, "That would be very nice." He sat down and the sergeant got into the refrigerator and served him a drink of iced coffee and made him a fruit drink and then a fancy salad. We did have fruit salad that night, but not arranged as fancily as that one. The major was obviously very thankful for that and after he had eaten it he looked around and saw me scrubbing away out there. He came out on the floor and said, "Well, soldier, what are you doing?" I said, "I am putting the finishing touches on the cleanup, this noon's cleanup." He said, "How do you like the food here?" and I said, "Oh, it's fine. We all like it very much. It's very good every day, sir." The sergeant was standing in the background beaming and the major said, "That's good. That's what we like to hear." Then he rubbed his thumb on the table and he went over and rubbed his thumb on the windowsill and that was the inspection. He said, "Sergeant, things look good," and he walked out. We got the pennant the third time around. After that inspection the sergeant took me back into his private room at the back of the kitchen and I had a cool drink and a fruit salad.

We got a break in the afternoon, each afternoon, and we would go outside, lounge around, have a smoke or whatever. I got exploring out back of the barracks in an area that had been an old open field and I discovered large numbers of a very big jumping spider, much bigger than we had in Maine. I got a gallon jar from the kitchen and captured one of these and put some twigs and grass in with him and then got grasshoppers to put in to watch his technique in catching them. Some of the fellows got interested in this and they were catching bugs and putting them in. The sergeant came out and wanted to know what was going on and I showed him. He was greatly taken with this and when the time came for us to go back to work, although I had intended to liberate the spider at that point, the sergeant took the jar, spider and all, back to his quarters. I think he kept it as a pet – it sort of fit his personality. I continued to get on well with him the rest of the time and rather enjoyed KP because it was a lot more comfortable than drilling out in the field in temperatures that would range into the nineties.

Then came the end of the training session. I think it was about eight weeks and I was assigned as barracks guard one day. That consisted of sitting around, outside preferably. It was cooler in the shade. I kept the fire going in the boiler that provided hot water for the showers when the troops came in. It was more of a job than it might seem because the coal used was that very soft southern coal that melted while burning and formed tremendous clinkers which had to be removed every now and then from the firebox. There were two elbows in the smoke pipe. It was rather dark in there and I stashed away two crullers that I was saving. I sat outside in a chair under the shade of adjacent trees reading a little book I had purchased on a trip into town, a collection of poetry by Sara Teasdale.

Basic Training

Pretty soon I noticed it was time to get the thing fired up so there would be plenty of hot water for the incoming troops. I went inside and opened the drafts and got things blazing away, but I noticed that I still wasn't getting the draft I wanted. I thought probably there had been an accumulation of soot in the elbows of the smoke pipe, so I went and beat on them with the poker. In the darkness in there I didn't notice that apparently they were rusted badly and I had made a hole in one of them. I went back out and returned to my book but pretty soon noticed smoke coming out of the door. I rushed in and rescued my crullers, and then pulled the alarm. The post fire station was quite close and they came immediately and got things under control, although those barracks, which were made of southern pitch pine and very dry, blazed up fiercely for a while. Just about then the troops returned from the field and the lieutenant of course wanted the report as to what was going on. I told him and he was furious. He accused me of lighting the fire myself and then asked me, "What was the first thing you did when the fire started?" By that time I was pretty angry at him, but I stayed calm and said, "Sir, I went inside and rescued the crullers that I had stashed in there." Well, of course that made him more furious than ever and he said, "What were you doing anyway during the afternoon here?" And I said, "When I wasn't stoking the fire I was reading poetry of Sara Teasdale." He said, "Poetry? I'm going to have you court martialed for gross negligence and I can think of some other things, too, like destruction of government property." And he went on.

Then he rushed me over to the company headquarters and requested the company commander to court martial me.

The company commander calmed him down and then asked me some questions about what had happened. He told the lieutenant that he didn't think there were grounds for a court martial, but he would like to talk to me privately about it and so he sent the lieutenant and everyone else off. He told me that the training period was all over and it sounded as if I had not done anything that was deliberately wrong. He asked me if I had heard of the ASTP program, and I said I had not. That was the Army Specialized Training Program and he asked me whether I knew French and I said, "Well, I can't say I really know French, but I've studied it both in high school and college and I can read it reasonably well." He said, "You should apply to the French branch of the ASTP program and I've got the forms right here." He had me make the application forthwith, and I was submitted to examination, passed it and was admitted to the program all in a matter of a day or so. That was the last day of the training and the lieutenant, trying to show that he was at heart all sweetness and light, invited all of the men to join him in a little party in town that Saturday night, with him as host. By that time the feelings between him and me were pretty chilly and I was the only one who didn't go.

II

Special Training

To begin the ASTP program I shipped out to the Georgia Teacher's College in Collegeboro, Georgia. This was in the early fall. They started by giving us an examination that was designed to eliminate those who were just too low on the learning scale for the program. I passed this all right. However, I decided that I was going to have to get some special tutoring if I was going to continue in this program because looking around I saw that many of the fellows were considerably older, many of them had masters degrees already, some even doctorates, and there were graduates of European universities. Many of them were exiles from Europe and I could see that I was a very junior member of this bunch. But, I had made acquaintance with a young Jewish native of Alexandria, Egypt who had a degree from the Sorbonne (the University of Paris), and I persuaded him to be my tutor so I would at least have a chance of passing the next elimination exam, which was scheduled in a couple of weeks. He was willing. We worked it out and he was an excellent tutor – a highly eccentric individual – but he taught me a good deal in a hurry and I studied very fiercely and passed the next elimination exam. That got me well into the program.

Christmastime came around. I spent it at St. Augustine and then came New Year's. A newly-made friend and I went to the Oglethorpe Hotel in Georgia for the extended holiday weekend. His name was Drew. He was a graduate of Yale and had spent some of his early teen years in Japan where he picked up a general knowledge of the language. He had now become a student of Japanese language and culture and was in the special program designed for that.

We went out to the hotel and got settled in. We had our books to study, his in Japanese, mine in French, and I think it was the second day we were there that we were out strolling around. We couldn't go on the beach because it was blocked by barbed wire and patrolled by a sentry. The hotel, a luxury resort hotel in normal times, was given over to the military at this point. We came in from our walk and the manager spoke to us saying, "There are two gentlemen who would like to see you in my office." We went in and the two gentlemen identified themselves as FBI officers and began to question us. It seems the housekeeper had found our books in our room and had reported to the manager that there were what appeared to be two foreign agents in the hotel, one probably Japanese, and he immediately called the FBI. We had some difficulty in assuring them that we were nothing of the sort. They had never heard of the ASTP program, but we persuaded them to call our headquarters at the teacher's college, which they did and finally got the matter straightened out. However, for the rest of our stay at Oglethorpe Hotel, we were aware of being watched closely by the hotel personnel and two or three times we caught some of the housemaids peering around corners at us. But nothing untoward happened and we went back to our courses.

While I was there I got news from home, in a letter that contained a newspaper clipping, that my old high school

Special Training

buddy, Bud Ellis, who had left high school to go directly into the Air Corps and had become a pilot of a P38, had been killed over Corsica during the African invasion. That was a sad day indeed for me.

When the program was completed at Georgia Teacher's College, shortly after New Year's, the French section was sent to Boston University. The program at Boston University was very rigorous, much more so than in Georgia, and was taught by exiled professors, mostly Jewish men from Europe. It involved not only the French language, but also all things French – French culture, art, and history, both political and social. One of the instructors, however, was a Swiss immigrant, an electrical engineer now in retirement who had helped design some of the mountain electric railways in Switzerland before the War. He was now living in Lincoln, Massachusetts and one of his sons, Jean Claude Donald Michel, had been at Bowdoin College with me. M. Michel was a delightful person. He taught us conversational French and was a great source of information. I think he was the one I enjoyed most. The professors were so grim in their determination to teach us what we were supposed to be taught that it was a little hard to get to know them very much.

We were bunked in the old Mechanics Hall complex in Boston. That was right out next to the railway in the Back Bay. They were fantastic buildings. We were on different levels and on balconies. We were all over the place and the Army of course called an inspection one day and we had to stay by our beds with them turned down so they could see the sheets. They delayed the inspection so long that four or five trains went by and for every one that went by, soot leaked into the building so every bed was besmirched with soot and there was a general flunking of the inspection. We had a great deal to say about the lack of any sense at all on the part of the inspecting officer.

The program went on until about early April, when those in charge realized that France was not going to need any military government, which is what we were being trained for. It was felt that they would be able to govern themselves. The program dissolved and after a leave which permitted us to go home for a break, we were all sent back into the infantry for a new round of basic training. This was to take place in Camp Picket, Virginia, made up of a group not only of us, but also of excess Air Corps enlisted men, and a lot of other miscellaneous personnel whom the Army decided were no longer needed in their special categories. So we were all popped back into the infantry, all made privates first class and ordered to receive basic training all over again.

We did have the advantages of being put in an organized division, the 78th Lightning Division. This made it much better than the initial basic training had been because we could get frequent leaves and other privileges that we hadn't had as basic trainees. The Army pulled a real blunder in sending us to the 78th division because the cadre was made up of old soldiers, mostly from the deep south and most of them had virtually no education outside the Army. All of us, on the other hand, from whatever program we came, were largely college and technical school graduates. We soon formed the impression that they were primitives, while they formed the impression of us that we were what would now be called hopeless nerds. The result was that they and we mixed like oil and water and the whole training session that went on all that summer in 1944 was pretty much a disaster. In fact, at the end of it we had maneuvers with several other divisions and we came out at the bottom of the list. We flunked officially, as a result of which they broke up the division and sent us all overseas as casual replacements, the significance of which I will come to later in this story.

III

Basic All Over Again

Right at the beginning a funny thing happened. I had been back in basic training only a few days when I was sent over to the officers' mess to wait on tables, a task for which I'd had no experience. I arrived there in the middle of the forenoon when some officers came in on a break. There was a full colonel, a lieutenant colonel and a major. They sat down and ordered coffee. I went into the kitchen and got hot coffee and brought it out. I had served the two colonels and the major was sitting on the other side of the table. I went around the table to serve him, tripped and spilled the hot coffee in his lap. I figured I was up for court martial. It also appeared from what developed that the colonels did not much like the major.

The colonel – the full colonel – began to laugh and the major was fuming, of course, but before he could say anything to me the colonel had begun to laugh, and then the lieutenant colonel began to laugh. Well, with them laughing at the incident the major couldn't very well fume at me. I apologized, of course, and the mess sergeant came rushing out of the kitchen with a mop and rags and did his best to dry off the major, who fumed and fussed in silence. They were in nicely starched suntan uniforms. The mess sergeant took me into the kitchen and said, "You're discharged! Go back to your company and tell them never to send you over here again." He apparently relayed the same message to my commanding officer. I got back to my company and the first sergeant said, "What in hell did you do over there? Did you shoot somebody?" I said, "No," and told them what had happened. They thought it was hilarious. That gave me a little lesson in how the Army operates, also.

One advantage of being in a regular division was that we could get leaves with some frequency on weekends, either in the local town or more distant ones. I visited at various times in Richmond and Washington, D.C. and two or three other closer places. I did some sightseeing and on one occasion, on a visit to Richmond, I was sightseeing with another group, all from New England, and a nice lady from an organization that was working to show soldiers hospitality was showing us around. She was working through the service club, I guess, and she took us, apparently without any self-consciousness or without realizing really what she was doing, down to what had been a notoriously bad prison during the Civil War in which many northern soldiers had died. She was explaining about the prison and we were all rather bemused when one of our men spoke up and said, "Madam, do you realize that everyone of this group you're talking to is from New England, many from Massachusetts." She suddenly stopped, she looked shocked and sputtered a bit and said, "Oh, well, let's move on to the next place. I'm sorry, I didn't realize what I was doing."

Virginia in April was lovely with dogwood in bloom, fruit trees blossoming, shrubs blossoming, masses of bloom everywhere. The air was scented, warm without being uncomfortably hot, moderate humidity, altogether a lovely place to be. We settled in at Camp Picket and started our basic training cycle all over again. It turned out to be a pretty boring procedure. One advantage, however, was that being in a regular division we were able, as I said, to get fairly frequent leaves to visit either the nearby town or a whole weekend leave to go to more distant places which, nevertheless, were easily reachable, like Richmond and Washington, D.C. I soon found that in these cities by going to the right bar one could get invited to the parties where the action was and this was a diversion that was much welcomed as an escape from the rigors of military training during the week. I met a number of interesting people in this way. So life went on there and then a ridiculous situation arose.

On one of my excursions I picked up a case of crabs, a sort of louse familiar to all the military. As an immediate measure I used the emergency treatment commonly used in the Army, the powerful lye soap used to scrub the floors in the barracks. This eliminated most of them, but I wanted to make sure. So I went on sick call and hoped to get some of the blue ointment, so-called, that was used for treating those little critters. The sergeant examined me and didn't find any and said, "Soldier, what makes you think you have crabs?" I said, "Well, I did have, but I probably washed them all away." He said, "Well, just wait here." He went in the other room to the doctor and reported to him, apparently, that there was a soldier outside who claimed to have crabs but didn't seem to have any. The doctor ordered me to come in. He was an officer, of course. Meanwhile I had examined myself and found one. I captured it and put it down on the doctor's desk on the pad of paper he had in front of him and I said, "See, sir? There it is. There is one." You would have thought I had put down a poisonous serpent in front of him. He was a big man and he reared back in his swivel chair and shouted at the sergeant. "Sergeant, get that thing out of here." And then he looked at me and said, "You are discharged for the day here." He said, "You can get back to your outfit and the sergeant will give you some blue ointment." I thought it was all over then, but it wasn't.

A couple of days later my sergeant said to me, "Richie, what's going on?" He said, "We have an order for you to see the regimental psychiatrist." I knew what that meant. I tramped more than halfway across camp to get to the psychiatrist and waited around for some time with a lot of other soldiers doing the same thing. When I went before him he was a cheerful gentleman who asked me a few questions and said to wait around awhile as he would probably ask me some more. All in all, I spent an hour or so there without having accomplished anything. With the march over there and the march back and the time spent waiting there it killed half a day. That suited me because it got me out of drill and they instructed me that I was to return every week at the same time for the indefinite future. I did that and pretty soon the group of us there who were patients formed a little social club that met on our own time at the service club where we were joined by the chief medic from the psychiatrist's office. He explained to us what the story was.

It seems the psychiatric program was new and the psychiatrist had to prove that he was really needed and so the more patients he had coming, the more that tended to prove he was needed and that's the way it went. We all were locked in a sort of little conspiracy. It favored us because once a week we got half a day off and also we were introduced to our colleagues there among the patients, many of whom – in fact most of whom – were very interesting people. As a result we had a very active social group at the service club. At the end of the term of our training we had a party at the service club. We had our own table where we met and we would get dubious glances from the fellows at neighboring tables who would look over and say, "Oh, that's those psychos over there." We got a kick out of that. We decided at our final party to really shake them up. We arranged to have drinks all around. Most of the guys were having their low alcoholic beer, but we ordered strawberry ice-cream sodas. That nearly caused a riot. I'll never forget it, but we came out unscathed and greatly enjoyed the experience.

Among the friends I met there was Nicky from Boston. He was a Harvard graduate, a portly young man, very witty, who later became a journalist, and we spent a lot of time together. There were others, too, and we enjoyed satirizing each other's little quirks, none of which were very serious and all in all it turned out to enliven the summer quite a good deal.

IV

To Combat

The Special Training program had been a lucky situation for us, because by getting caught up in this program we had escaped participation in D-day, which otherwise probably would have encompassed us. After a short home leave, we shipped out of New York on the *Île de France*, which was one of the luxury liners of the day comparable to the English Queens, the *Queen Mary* and the *Queen Elizabeth*. Like them, the *Île de France* traveled alone because of its speed and maneuverability. And it was armed. It had an English naval gun on the stern with an English gun crew and several Y guns on the upper deck that fired depth charges.

We headed out taking the northern route across the Atlantic in September bound for England. Everything went along smoothly at first. The ship was jammed with 12,000 people, I was told. The enlisted men like myself were way down in the hold. We were slowly graded upward according to rank with the officers in cabins near the top. The top deck of cabins was for the women personnel. When we reached our destination the WACS and the WAVES were largely confined to rear area operations, office workers especially. The nurses, however, often got into areas of danger.

The crossing progressed. I had taken along two or three books, paperbacks that included Shakespeare's history plays. I'd been a student of Shakespeare in college and I wanted to reread the history plays, which I did in the course of the voyage.

Halfway over we had an alarm. The ship sighted a submarine or submarines, or detected them in the water beneath the ship, and suddenly it turned a full right angle turn, shifting to top speed from its cruising speed. The top speed for the *Île de France* was way up in the thirty-mile-an-hour range and for the submarines in those days, underwater top speed was about nine miles an hour. Even on the surface it wasn't much more than eleven, I guess. Immediately depth charges were fired. The ship took a course due south. There was a map on the wall of the dining area on which the daily progress of the ship was marked and the new course was apparent on the map within a few hours. Also, traveling in a great ship like that you don't actually hear the engines, but you become aware of a fine vibration. It becomes so much a part of your daily being that you don't really notice it unless there's a change. When the speed was shifted from cruising to full speed, we felt it right off. We felt the ship dig in. It was quite exciting. Everyone was very excited about it. We were warned not to get over excited. We were given a particular warning that should anything occur, or should we sight anything, we should not all gather on one side of the ship. There were so many people it could cause it to heel dangerously.

For two full days, I think, we headed due south. We got into the warm waters of the gulf stream and people were sunbathing. It was beautiful weather and the submarines apparently had been left well behind. Then we swung around and headed straight for Ireland going up through the Irish Sea to Greenock, the port of Glasgow. When we got just about in sight of Ireland we were given a British escort of gunboats.

During the voyage we had to entertain ourselves. The feeding started about 6:00 in the morning and we had only two meals because it took over half a day to feed everybody once, and as soon as we finished the first feeding, the second one began and there was a PX on board where we could get snacks. With such a horde of people, it was a little disconcerting until you got used to it.

We made it to Greenock without any further incidents, disembarked, and were put on trains that headed south through Scotland and England. We made it virtually nonstop all the way to the south coast of England. As we went through cities we passed through commercial areas pretty much and workers, largely women, would come to the windows and wave at us. The word had gotten out, apparently. We got to the region of Southampton in the south of England and were there for only a day or so and then loaded on a transport to France. By this time, September 1944, the fighting had moved across France. Paris had been liberated in August and the troops had come pretty much to a halt at the Siegfried line along the border of Germany, Belgium, Luxembourg and France. We were landed at Omaha Beach, which was still strewn with the wreckage of the D-day landing, and then transported inland some distance and put into a camp for sorting out.

From there we went to a more northern area in France for an interlude, waiting to be further sorted out and shipped out as replacements. This particular location – and I don't know where it was – was in a sort of romantic way a timeless interlude in my journey. We were encamped in a huge park on the grounds of an eighteenth-century chateau which was still inhabited, the proprietor being an officer in the French army away on his duties. However, still in the chateau was his young son, about twelve years old. He was very much lord of the manor. He would come out to us two or three times a day on his pony visiting the troops and was very popular. He was a very personable boy and in spite of his lordly manner gladly accepted gifts of chocolate and other candy that the troops willingly passed to him.

The grounds were under huge trees. I think they must have gone back to the eighteenth century. There were great oaks and beeches and nearby was what was left of what had once been an ornamental basin still filled with water, but also with water plants and a lot of weeds. Around it on one side was a ruin that had been an artificial ruin, I would say, as was the style in the eighteenth century in many places, like the remnants of a Greek temple. Here and there among the trees there were statues in classic style. The whole thing was dreamlike. The men played games and wrestled and generally tried to take up the time. One evening we had a performance of *Oklahoma!* that seemed peculiarly out of place in that setting, the backdrop being one wall of the chateau. It was one of the visiting theatrical companies from the States.

Eventually we moved on from there. Before we left, having found the woods were full of mushrooms of various kinds, I took a little pocket notebook that I had and filled it with descriptions and drawings of the mushrooms. I'm sorry to say I lost it somewhere along the way.

Soon we were moved up still farther to another replacement camp and this one was closer to the Seigfried Line. The first night there we were encamped in shallow foxholes with just a "shelter half" – half a pup tent – over us. We were strafed by a German plane that made a sudden assault. It was a single plane, a single pass. There were a number of casualties, but I was not injured and we moved on.

The final sorting out was just a few miles behind the lines. We could hear action in the distance and the personnel who were sorting us out were obviously very nervous. So were we. We lined up and the roll was read. They'd ship us out by truckloads in two-and-a-half-ton trucks. I forget how many men in each truck, twenty maybe. I was there lined up with the others and all of a sudden I just passed out completely. I can only ascribe it to the nervous tension. They carried me off to the medics' tent, brought me around and the medical officer made me lie there for a bit.

Meanwhile, the group had been shipped out to the front lines. When I'd come around enough I was sent back out and the officer who was lining everybody up bawled me out saying, "Should have been on the first shipment. Why weren't you here?" And so on and so forth. I didn't know what to say. I told him, "Well, sir, I passed out." He apparently either didn't hear me or paid no attention. He was obviously very upset for various reasons. "No excuse," he said, and at that point I was saved by the medical officer who stepped in and said, "I beg your pardon, Captain, but do you know this man was unconscious when the group went out? He was physically unable to know what was going on." Then the officer said, "All right, so he's in the next group." I was shipped out in the next truckload. That was lucky for me because as it turned out the truckload I would have been on was shipped straight into combat and several of them never even got a chance to fire a gun before they were killed.

We were at the edge of the great battle of the Huertgen Forest, one of the nastiest, deadliest and most furious battles in the War and one that has not gotten the publicity that it probably should have. Modern historians tell us it was a totally unnecessary battle, but it went on from then until December 16th when the Battle of the Bulge began.

I went up with the sergeant and the group, a dozen or so, and we were greeted by a second lieutenant. The sergeant said, "Lieutenant, where's the rest of the company?" and the lieutenant said, "This is it." There was just a lieutenant and about sixty men left in the company, which normally would have six officers and about a hundred and sixty men. The lieutenant said, "Find a foxhole. There are plenty of them around. Get in and stay there until morning."

On the first day of duty we were permitted to have breakfast, and we had some hot breakfast I'm glad to say, because the company – what was left of it – had been pulled back to the rear in order to be re-manned and re-equipped. We were assigned four men to a blanket and sent out through the dense spruce woods, to pick up American bodies. The fighting had been fierce and it had ranged back and forth for a week or so, first the Germans on top and then the Americans. Bodies were everywhere, German and American, and we were instructed to pick up only the American.

In many cases the bodies had been lying there a week or more. They were swollen from the internal gasses of decay.

They were slate gray in color and they stank. Rigor mortis had set in. As many of them had died in distorted positions from the pain and anguish, getting them on a blanket and carrying them on a blanket was a major operation, physically very demanding. Emotionally, also. Some of the men wept, some of them vomited and I had a little conference with myself to the effect that if I was going to last at all in this thing I was going to have to shut my feelings away in a back room of my mind and lock them up. And that's what I did.

By noontime we had built up a stack of bodies about the equivalent in size and looking somewhat like two cords of wood, and we covered these with a tarpaulin along the edge of a firebreak to be picked up by the grave registration people later on. By that time it had been a long morning and I was hungry. I found I had a good appetite in spite of it all, and most us, except for a few who were overcome, sat down beside our cord of bodies and had lunch from our rations. In the afternoon we repeated the operation and managed to clean up all the bodies we could find in that particular area.

These spruce woods were quite old. They must have been planted before World War I as part of the West Wall, so called – a German fortification. The trees were big European spruce from which the branches spread out and the foliage drooped. It rained with great frequency. In fact, from about the time I got there it rained twenty-eight consecutive days, for various amounts of time each day, the sun hardly showing at all. It was miserable. We were wet all the time. We were constantly subject to attacks of mortar shells and 88 mm cannon coming in. The shells from the 88s used fuses that fired them when they came into the trees and before they got to the ground. Proximity shells they were called. We used them too. They would explode and the ground would be showered not only with the shrapnel from above, but with masses of tree limbs. We found that one of the best ways of defending against this was to literally hug trees, to hug the trunks of the trees. Nevertheless, the casualties were very heavy. You rarely saw the enemy because of the fire from the artillery and mortars.

The roads going through that forest were largely mud. They were narrow and they were crooked. Tanks were useless. They couldn't get off the roads because of the forest, and every curve was covered by a pillbox with a cannon in it. It was suicide for tanks to fight in there. So it came down to the infantry and we fought by patrols, small groups of men under a sergeant's command going out and fighting guerrilla style, back and forth in the woods, utterly miserable fighting.

At night we had listening posts. Three of us would be put in a big foxhole outside the main defense line, and we were supposed to be there all night listening. We couldn't leave once we got there because booby-traps were put up in the form of hand grenades about chest high on the trees in food cans into which they just fit with the pin drawn. The food can held down the handle that would trigger the explosion, and they were strung together with a wire. In the darkness if something tripped that wire, it would pull the grenade out of the can and explode it. We were connected to our own headquarters only by a sound power telephone. These were used very widely in the War. It was a small telephone and a fine wire and when you spoke into the phone it was energized. They were quite effective over a short distance. I was in one of these outposts for several nights and it was pretty miserable. We were supposed to be two men on and one sleeping for two-hour shifts, and of course the two on couldn't make any noise. We had to listen for any odd noises. In the woods at night there are many noises you can hear even if there are no enemy near. I worked out some ways of enduring it.

One way was to rehearse music that I knew. A college friend of mine, who had gotten into the Army a year or two before I did, said, "Listen to a lot of music before you go in." I did anyway. My taste is classical music, ironically German classical music. I listened to a lot of Brahms and Mozart. I would sit there in the darkness in the silence listening, and in my head trying to recapture long passages of a Brahms symphony. I did remarkably well, too, better than I ever was able to at any other time.

One night I was put in a listening post with a young fellow from Kentucky. I don't know what his name was. He was called Kentuck by everybody. He was only nineteen, but he was a devoted soldier and a tough guy. And along with us was a recruit who had just arrived from a suburb of New York City and obviously, as was true of many of the men who were coming in at that time, very poorly trained. They were hurrying them in because they were getting short of men.

This boy was about eighteen and he was already terrified before he ever got there. We were given our orders and we had hardly settled down when he began to whimper. Kentuck told him he would have to keep quiet, but he'd still whimper and get louder rather than quieting down. Kentuck got a little rough with him, grabbed him by the arm, shook him and told him to shut up. He slapped his face, but nothing would seem to quiet him down for long. He'd quiet down at first and then begin to whimper again. He got worse and worse until finally Kentuck reported back to the CO on the sound phone who said, "Well, there's nothing we can do now until dawn. You'll have to make the best of it." We made the best of it by further trying to impress on this boy that he must be quiet. When he didn't we put him face down on one of the blankets there and sat on him, but that didn't help very much.

When the boy got louder than ever, Kentuck got absolutely disgusted and he drew from his boot holster sheath the combat knife that all infantrymen were issued. It was polished and sharpened to perfection and he put it to the boy's throat, got a grip on the boy's shoulders and said, "Look here, you either be quiet or I'm going to cut your throat." He sounded as if he meant it, and knowing him, I think he did. The boy then fell quiet and he looked at me. I just looked away because I agreed with Kentuck. A little time went on and then the boy broke down again. Kentuck grabbed him this time, put the knife to his throat and I saw some drops of blood run down. I said, "For God's sake don't really cut his throat." Kentuck said, "By God, I'll cut his head off if he doesn't shut up." The boy then became absolutely terrified and I think he actually passed out because he was silent for quite a long time lying on the floor of the hole. It was evident that none of us were going to get any sleep that night.

A couple more times the boy came to and began getting upset again. A couple more times he got threatened and the night went on like that until finally came the dawn. The nights are very long in the autumn at that latitude. When we went back to the company, the boy completely broke down, was hysterical and had to be shipped out to the medics. He never came back. I've often wondered whether he ever actually recovered from that night, terrified as he was before ever seeing the enemy.

Time went on. One of the things that never seems to get across in movies and shows about the War and combat is one of the worst aspects of it. In a situation such as we had in the Huertgen Forest, it is not so much the individual events during a day that are bad, but the fact that they go on day after day after day. It's the duration that is killing. You greet each day with a feeling of absolute misery, "Oh no, not another one." You've got to go slogging on another day and then you do – most do – although some didn't. Men broke down with some frequency and had to be shipped out to the medics. Sometimes they came back and sometimes they didn't.

One day things were particularly miserable. We had suffered heavy casualties again and had been pulled back into a rear position, still in the woods. It was raining. Trees were dripping. We were wet and cold and miserable. Our platoon lieutenant came out with his liquor ration and was joined by the platoon sergeant. In World War II the officers – at least in Europe – got a regular liquor ration. It came over from England. In this case it was choice stuff. He had a bottle of Teacher's Highland Cream scotch and he offered any of us a drink who wanted it. Under those conditions a shot of scotch was very, very welcome and most all of us took one. I think the lieutenant saved only one for himself.

Another thing happened that was to have an interesting future result. We were pulled back from the front one day to receive reinforcements and supplies, including a hot lunch, which had been rather unusual. They brought up hot lunch from the rear in huge thermos tins. I had finished mine and there was a period when we had nothing to do. Down through the woods I heard someone whistling, of all things, the opening bars of Mozart's 40th Symphony in G minor and he repeated it several times. I thought to myself in astonishment that the likelihood of an American GI whistling Mozart is remote indeed, but it can't be a German. We were back in a reserve area and our troops were all through the woods. I determined to find out what was going on. I walked down through the woods repeating the theme, which happens to be one I knew well because that symphony is one of my favorites. When I got down there he echoed me and I echoed him until we found each other. It was the headquarters company encampment and the whistler was a fellow named Jack, the radio man for the company headquarters. He had been a graduate student at Cornell University and had been the classical disc jockey on the university radio station. We got acquainted right away and remained close for the rest of the War. It was a great discovery because he was a remarkably congenial companion and later on, when we had more free time at the end of the War, we got to know each other very well.

One weapon that we were all very leery about was the buzz bomb. The first of the German secret weapons were flying bombs. They were big bombs with wings and a little jet engine on top and they made a buzzing sound coming along at a low altitude, low enough so they sometimes could be shot down by rifle fire. However, they also were very erratic and although they were fired at England, they oftentimes fell into the combat area. If one hit it was devastating because the thing blasted on the surface of the ground and if it landed in the woods, it would create a great open area with all the trees leaning outward from where the center of the explosion occurred. If one landed in a manned area, as one did in our weapons company one day, it was a catastrophe. It killed a lot of the men, injured a lot of others and destroyed some of the weapons. So when we heard one of them going over, the inclination was to hold your breath. If the engine cut out, watch out.

Being in the Huertgen Forest was like being in hell. Every day, day after day, the same grind. Attack, retreat, or rather withdraw, I should say. The American Army never retreats. It makes "strategic withdrawals." Battling back and forth over the same ground, more men get killed, more men get injured, new men come up. Old officers go. New officers come up. Still no progress. You don't know what's going on outside your area. We don't know who is winning the war. We don't know why we're in there or whether we'll ever get out. It's the most miserable aspect of war. Perhaps it was good for me that the worst time I spent in the whole seven months or more I was in combat was right at the start, with one important exception.

The unit to which I had been sent was Company B of the 60th Infantry Regiment of the 9th Infantry Division. According to the official record, the 9th Infantry Division during the Battle of the Huertgen Forest had 3,836 casualties. Toward the end of October, the 9th Infantry Division was thought to be so battered that it needed an extended rest and we were moved to the rear. They had established a rest camp back around Camp Elsenborn which was somewhat to the rear. I was able to get sent back there, having already spent what was considered a long time in combat for a foot soldier. We could get hot showers, new uniforms, have time – several days – to see movies and eat hot food and generally rest. It was much needed by all of us. I didn't realize what tension I had built up inside me during that period in the Huertgen Forest.

I got back there. I got my new uniform. I had a hot shower and was dressing to go downstairs to supper. We were in an old hotel there. All of a sudden it hit me. I collapsed on the bed. I couldn't stop crying. I shook. I was in an awful state. Fortunately, the man who was sharing the room with me, whom I didn't know, but who was a veteran soldier, saw what was happening and he went down to the bar and got me a stiff drink and brought it up. That did the trick. In a few minutes I was able to calm down, get a grip on myself and go downstairs. There was no repetition of that attack. I enjoyed the supper. I saw a movie, and in general got well rested. That sort of thing is a lifesaver under those conditions. A new chapter was about to open and it would contain the worst hours of all the time I spent in combat.

V

To the Roer

We finally struggled out of the Huertgen Forest and began heading toward the Roer River. Many outfits were going in the same direction. The Roer was the site of several dams, which if the Germans opened them could flood large areas of the countryside down below that would have greatly interfered with our advance. We went through several villages and experienced several minor skirmishes until we approached the Roer River opposite the city of Dueren, which is on the easterly side. We rested that night in a brickyard. My lieutenant wanted me to be his runner and I consented to this not realizing at the time the risks I was undertaking. Generally, the runners had a short operational life because they were often out moving around during the action. However, the lieutenant urged me to do it. He didn't order me, but he asked me to do it and I consented. It appealed to me because I've always been somewhat of a lone operator, as the runner has to be, and for this very reason it was not a popular function among most of the men who preferred the teamwork of the regular squad operation.

The lieutenant's name was Reardon. He was from Michigan and this was his third time up. He had been wounded out twice before and his nerves were pretty well shot. He realized this and he was very much afraid, as he made apparent to me, that he would get so nervous and jittery that he would do something foolish and expose either himself or the men to excessive danger. He asked me to spend the night with him in a brick kiln in the brickyard. Neither one of us could sleep very much so we made use of candle-making materials that the Germans had left there and made candles for a good part of the night while having conversation. He did most of the talking. I was a good listener and I found this a valuable asset in dealing with later platoon lieutenants whom I would serve. Finally, we got a little sleep and the next morning as soon as it got light we got ready to go.

There was a wide front where the whole battalion was involved, but we had a central area opening on a broad field, a garden actually, beyond which were a large factory and a town. I think it was Marienweiler. The day was intermittently rainy, the ground muddy, and we got off to a bad start because the opening of the attack was supposed to have been preceded by a barrage from our heavy artillery several miles in the rear. However, the heavy artillery got bogged down somewhere back there and we didn't get the barrage. We moved forward anyway, the infantry following the tanks. We got well out into the gardens and found that intelligence had fallen down on the job also. Right across the middle of the gardens was a big irrigation ditch and it was a very big one. It was at least fifteen feet wide and it must have been eight feet deep. The only fortunate thing about it was there was very little water in it. The tanks could not cross this and they couldn't sit out there as targets themselves so they swung around and headed back leaving us exposed. We already had been under fire to some degree from the time we started and now we were wide open moving forward in a frontal assault, the worst kind. Thus began the day that was to be I think the worst day of my life.

We carried on and were approaching that big irrigation ditch when at the far side of the field, several haystacks, or so we thought they were, burst apart and we found that they contained hidden tanks, mortars and machine gun nests. All of these opened up full blast at us and they were only about a hundred and fifty yards away. I was going along at the prescribed distance of about five yards from the lieutenant and a little to his rear and to his left. To my left was the platoon sergeant, about another five yards left and ahead of me. Lieutenant Reardon went down, the platoon sergeant went down and I hit the earth, although I wasn't hit.

We all hit the earth and began crawling toward the irrigation ditch. The heavy fire was tremendous. I had just gotten to the edge of the ditch when a mortar shell hit nearby and although none of the shrapnel touched me, the concussion knocked me into the ditch and stunned me for a few seconds. I came to with one of my buddies shaking my shoulder saying, "Richie, Richie, are you dead? Are you dead?" And I mumbled, "No, I'm not dead yet." Then I got myself together and went to the lieutenant. He was sitting, his back against the sloping sides of the ditch with that vacant, remote look in his eyes that seemed to be characteristic of dying men. I comforted him as best I could. He wanted water. I held him in my arms and gave him a little sip of water. He wanted a cigarette and I held a cigarette between his lips. He puffed one long puff and he died. I laid him down. It took me a few minutes to recover from that.

The memory of making candles with Lieutenant Reardon, which formed the background of a sudden, intense friendship, followed the next day by the very fate that my new-found friend dreaded so, suggested the title for this book.

Although numb with fear, I summoned a fatalistic attitude and looked around to see what I could do. One man, his arm torn off by shrapnel, in his mortal agony screamed curses at God. Others writhing in the mud screamed to God to save them. Still others moaned away their lives. Terror of death was everywhere. Men looked with horror at their own wounds gushing blood, some weeping, some cursing. The scene was one of sickening chaos.

The ditch was filled with men wounded, crying for the medics, shouting this and that, but still crawling in from the garden, falling, rolling into the ditch. The water that ran in the bottom of it was a mixture of mud and blood. It was about the color of tomato bisque. We had had three medics in the company starting out. Two of them were wounded and out of action. The remaining one happened to be one that I had gotten to know well. A very small but husky young fellow about eighteen years old, he was working his head off trying to treat the wounded. I went to his aid, got the supplies from the wounded medics and brought them to him, then helped him as he administered shots to the wounded men or tried to patch them up as best he could, because they were going to have to wait there until after the fighting before any relief could take them out.

Many of them, badly wounded as they were, would thrash around and further injure themselves and I tried to hold them down while my medic buddy gave them their shot of morphine. The morphine came in little tubes, one shot each and each with its own needle. He would carry them in a kind of vest that he wore under his jacket to keep them warm and he would inject them one by one. The medics had a saying that one shot brought relief, two shots brought eternity. I was in a state of shock I think, doing things more or less automatically and I'd reached the conclusion that I probably would never get out of there alive. I gave my overcoat to a wounded man to make him more comfortable. I had decided that overcoats were no proper combat uniform anyhow and never wore one afterward, relying instead during the rough winter weather on several layers of clothing, adding a layer each time it got colder.

Mortar shells were landing all around, sometimes in the ditch, creating more havoc and injury and death. All of our officers except the executive officer who stayed in the rear were wounded or killed, and finally he came forward and took command. Sergeants were taking charge, those that were left. I think we hardly would have survived any of this had not the heavy artillery finally got into place sometime in the afternoon and opened fire on the enemy. After a bit of this the Germans retreated and began going over the bridge to the city of Dueren across the river.

We then rallied and, under the command of our surviving officer, came out of the ditch and rushed forward to the factory, taking cover inside the buildings. We were still under sporadic fire as the Germans withdrew and when they got well across the river they began firing their 88s and their heavier artillery from there. However, by nightfall we had established ourselves in the factory and set up defensive positions. I was in such a state of nerves that night that I was unable to lie down and could hardly sit down. I spent a great deal of the night walking around inside the building, only occasionally sitting down, until finally I was able to sit down and doze for awhile.

At one point early on, before it became completely dark, we discovered that we needed water. The factory's water supply had been cut by artillery fire, but the well was still functioning outside the building. A man went out to get water and a sniper that the Germans had left behind – as was their custom in village fighting – knocked him down. Another man tried a different route and the sniper knocked him down. So the sergeant said to me, "Richie, see what you can do about getting us some water." I was not about to be the third man to get knocked down by that sniper, so I did a little scouting to see if I could locate where the sniper was and I figured out where he had to be.

There was a brick tower on the back of the mill, which was an old building. It had been hit by a light artillery shell that had knocked out a window and a portion of the wall of the tower leaving a gaping hole there. All of the other windows were tightly shut and there seemed to be no place on the roof that a man could hide, so I assumed that he had to be behind that opening somewhere. I looked up a friend of mine who was particularly good at the use of rifle grenades. He went out with me and we carefully scouted around keeping out of sight as best we could until we got in a suitable position. Then he fired a rifle grenade right through the middle of that hole. There followed a terrific explosion. Bricks and mortar, pieces of window and other things came flying out. I figured had there been a sniper in there, he was no longer alive, and scouting along the edge of the building and going from cover to cover as best I could, I got to the water and was able to bring back a jerry can full of it. I'm sure we got the sniper because we heard no more from him.

The next day reinforcements were brought up. Wounded men were carried out. What was left of our platoon, which wasn't much, the sergeant and a dozen men I guess, were posted into what had been the factory air-raid shelter as a sort of outpost. It was a massive building as the Germans built them with very thick walls. Two-thirds of it was underground and in it was the equipment including a big iron cook stove, a good supply of coal, dishes and so forth. We were supposed to stay there probably that day and one night. Sergeant says to me, "Richie, you are the cook," and I said, "Well, I'm sorry for you." But, they got cartons of "ten-in-one rations" to us. Those were rations in small cartons, waxed to make them waterproof. They contained quite a variety of highly concentrated food and were supposed to supply one man with rations for ten days or ten men for one day or any combination thereof. My approach was to take several cartons of those rations, dump all of the meat products into a huge skillet I found there – very much like the skillets you would find in an upstate Maine lumber camp – put it on the stove and cook up a big hash as the main item. That seemed to appeal to most everybody so I got it going and the smell of it was great. Everyone was ready.

Just about then the Germans pulled up a self-propelled 88 on the other side of the river and began zeroing in their shells right on the air-raid shelter. They wouldn't penetrate. That shelter must have been four feet thick with steel reinforced concrete. But, every time there was an explosion against the shelter, little flakes of concrete would peel off the inside of the ceiling and the walls. Some of them were falling into the hash which I had neglected to cover. I didn't know it and no one noticed it happening. The 88 quit. The 88s were on self-propelled mounts and they held a rack of eight shells. They would pull the self-propelled mount into a predetermined position, fire the eight shells in rather rapid succession and then pull out to another location before our heavy artillery could get zeroed in on them.

We gathered together to eat the hash. People began hoeing in. "Boy, isn't this great? Richie, you've done it." And just about then somebody said, "Richie, what have you done?" And they began to crunch on the little flakes of concrete. I think we ended up eating it anyway, but I never lived it down. Jokes would be made regarding Richie's concrete hash. Fortunately, we were relieved about midday and I didn't have to do any more cooking. What was left of us was pulled back and prepared for the next event.

This was the twelfth day of December 1944, a day that I have never forgotten and that I never want to repeat. There had been terrible sights that day. Our platoon staff sergeant had part of his hand shot off and he went screaming to the rear waving the bloody hand. Men fell wounded or dead. They were crushed under the tracks of tanks, or trampled into the mud by their buddies as they rushed for cover. That ditch must have presented a terrible sight when the graves registration people finally were able to get there because I remember well that when I left it it was almost solidly lined with bodies and blood.

As a result of this operation, my company, Company B of the 60th Infantry Regiment, received a presidential citation, which is rather a rarity for a small unit. They are frequently awarded, but usually to larger units. For a company to get one is quite unusual.

In retrospect, one of the more horrifying aspects of a battle such as we had just been through was something that was repeated over and over for the rest of the War, particularly during the winter when ground conditions were wet, snowy or muddy as they usually were. Bodies of the Germans were all over the place, but we just let them lie. I suppose afterward what was left of them was picked up by some cleanup unit. The combat units had neither time nor energy to bother with them. It was hard enough to pick up our own dead and wounded. But I got used to seeing them, those bodies lying in the mud, trampled, run over, hardly recognizable as human bodies anymore, just garbage really. It was pretty horrifying to think of that.

One of the pervasive odors was the smell of rotting flesh we frequently encountered. Another, the smell of cordite from the explosions of shells in the mud and earth would hang in the air for days. Those odors would hang over not only the battlefield but also large areas beyond where the intense fighting took place.

German villages still had their little village shops for a lot of common necessities. Paint shops for one, and they characteristically had dry pigments and mixed the paints to order. In one case, in a small village where there had been some heavy fighting, the paint shop was struck by a shell that exploded right in the middle of it. The result was that dry pigments scattered all over the surrounding area, which included a lot of dead Germans. Seeing these bodies twisted, distorted, mud covered, bloody, and covered with these fantastic colors, was like a scene out of a horror movie, a scene that I remember too well.

We were sent back to a rear area to re-group, to get re-inforcements, and to re-equip. We were in such terrible shape that it took several days. We got a new lieutenant to take Lieutenant Reardon's place. His name was Lieutenant Self. At this point I might say that the job of second lieutenant platoon leader in the infantry is, in my opinion, the worst job in the Army. He's a lonely man. His men look to him for leadership and also he has to be virtually a surrogate father, give advice on all kinds of things and there is no relief from that. If he makes any mistakes he is sat upon by his superior officers who are likely to blame him for everything that goes wrong. I heard about all this from my lieutenants. Lieutenant Self was an unfortunate example. He was a nice fellow, a young man with a background similar to mine. He had gone from college right into the Army and officer training school, but had been given a staff job. He had been on that assignment ever since he had been on active duty in Europe. Now suddenly, because of a shortage of lieutenants, he was thrust right into a combat platoon, a type of service for which he had had no practice whatsoever. He did not feel himself competent to handle it and this feeling quickly filtered down. There is nothing that will disturb and lower morale more quickly in an infantry platoon than for the men to feel that their lieutenant is not up to the job. They will begin to avoid him as much as they can and they actually become leery of being led by him if they feel he does not really know what he is doing.

To the Roer

Lieutenant Self was determined to make the right effort here. He was certainly personally brave, but as he told me, he felt insufficiently trained for what he was supposed to do and it gave him a feeling of bitterness and helplessness and a feeling that he was doomed. We were ordered into an operation that was headed toward the crossing of the Roer River right in the middle of December. We were shifted out and marched along a ridgeline highway. The night before I'd spent quite a long time with Lieutenant Self at his request, and he had talked to me a lot about his past, about his feelings, about his bitterness toward the Army. I came away with the gut feeling that Lieutenant Self was indeed destined to be killed shortly. He had the same feeling I think.

The next day we were marching along a ridge highway above the Roer River. I was very leery of the exposure I felt we were undergoing and I was keeping close to the ditch, about twenty yards behind the lieutenant. We were very exposed. The Germans did see us and opened up with 88s from across the river. One of them struck right on top of poor Lieutenant Self. He was obliterated. Hardly a trace of him remained. The same explosion that hit him, knocked me into the ditch and nearly drowned me in a flood of water and mud, but otherwise I was not injured. Everyone who had taken cover in the ditches escaped injury. There were the usual cries for medics and much confusion. It was already late in the day and visibility was poor. However, we pulled ourselves together and made our way to a pre-selected camping spot where in the darkness I was nearly run over by a truck.

VI

The Battle of the Bulge

The next day we were supposed to start procedures for crossing the river, but the word came down to us. It's all over. It's all off. We're being moved. At first we didn't understand what had happened, but finally the word came down. The Germans have made an attack. It was the beginning of the Battle of the Bulge, which we then called the Ardennes Breakthrough.

We hiked to a more sheltered area, boarded trucks, the faithful two-and-a-half-ton trucks, and were carried a considerable distance by a rather round about route back to an area we had become somewhat familiar with earlier, the town of Monschau. We were to establish and hold what became known as the Monschau pivot. That was the approximate location of the hinge of the northern corner of the breakthrough. It became a highly contested area with a great deal of fighting back and forth that would continue to be pretty much in the same area for several weeks, in fact until The Bulge finally collapsed near the end of January.

One incident occurred there that was quite interesting. While we were getting settled down reinforcing troops were sent up to us, and among them coming into our company was a fellow who became generally known simply as The Reverend. He was a young guy who was apparently the minister of a small splinter group of Southern Baptists – in

Alabama, I think it was. But that group was not recognized by the Army so he could have no official status. He was willing enough to do most anything, but he would not bear arms. The captain didn't know quite what to do with him but was sympathetic to him. So he went about the company doing this and that and helping out wherever he could. For a while he spent some time with our platoon and shared a foxhole with me. It was a big German-made hole roofed over with heavy timbers and quite comfortable, which was fortunate because we were under fire for three or four days in succession and virtually confined to our holes at least during the daylight hours. He was of course armed with his Bible and was one of those devoted Christian types who live from and by the Bible. I don't think he ever read anything else, and his education apparently had been almost entirely founded on the Bible, which he unquestionably knew very well.

I immediately presented a challenge to him, since I do not profess to be a Christian at all, but rather a pantheist with humanist ethical principles. What we set out to do, largely by candlelight, was to read the New Testament aloud. I would read for a while and then he would read for a while and so on. This went on for about three days. We read the entire New Testament and some of the Old. In the course of our reading we would stop and discuss various passages, me critically and he from his religious point of view. Needless to say when we were through neither one had much influenced the other, but we were good friends nevertheless. He was certainly very sincere in his point of view and I was serious in mine.

Later on he went and stayed for a while with one of the other platoons and sometimes with the headquarters group.

We in our platoon were shifted in our position so I lost track of him for awhile. Then there was some severe fighting and our old position was attacked by some German tanks. The captain and the Reverend, who was with him at the time, were run over and crushed by the tanks.

Christmas came, but there was a lot of action and we had little time or inclination to celebrate it. I had received a package from home, however, and it was quite a large box of my mother's molasses cookies. Mother's molasses cookies were famous during my childhood among my friends because they were made from a recipe that had come from her great-grandmother. I've never tasted any quite like them since, but they were very good. Everyone agreed to that and when I got this box I stashed a few of them in my pack and then carried the box around distributing them to the other members of the platoon. Needless to say I was jokingly referred to as Santa Claus for awhile. They lasted less than a day.

The weather had been very stormy, overcast and generally unpleasant, but about Christmas day it cleared and our Air Force was able to come over. There were some sharp fights in the sky right over us at one point and we were ordered into our holes because of falling fragments of red-hot metal which would hit in the wet snow and mud and hiss and steam. Two or three people were badly hurt when they got clipped by some of these. Nevertheless they were welcomed because of the damage to the other side.

On another occasion a V-2 rocket, one of those that were sent over London, landed outside of our area. However, it hit in some woods and fields and the only result was a big hole. No one was injured at all, although when it hit the shock was so great we thought we were having an earthquake. On another occasion the medic and I who were sharing a hole, which we had covered with an igloo of our own construction, got further snowed under during the night when there was a heavy storm. We had put a shelter half over the entrance to protect us from the storm, but so much snow drifted up against it that we couldn't get out. We had to be rescued by other members of our platoon.

On several occasions our regimental colonel visited the front, Colonel Van Houten. He was a kind of General Patton character on a lesser scale. We appreciated the visits, but we were a little afraid of them too because he would get up in full view of the enemy on occasion and draw enemy fire. He of course would withdraw, but we were left out there receiving the fire. Our cannon company, armed with its 105 mm cannon, fired day and night, so constantly that the guns were burned out and since we were under British command, under Marshall Montgomery at that time, a British gun crew came in with their guns. I think they called them 20 pounders and they fired away at the same constancy. We fired mortars and everything we had to keep the Germans from extending their lines northward and tried to constrict them as much as possible in their passage. We had not been taken by surprise and were well organized so we did not suffer anywhere near the damage as did those units which had been caught in the center of the Bulge.

One weapon that the Germans used widely and that we really hated was the knee mortar. A knee mortar was a small mortar firing a projectile smaller than a hand grenade. It had a base shaped to fit over a man's thigh. Some German mortar men became incredibly expert using these and could land one of those little mortar bombs practically in someone's back pocket. They were short range of course, but in short range fighting they could be pretty deadly. On one occasion one landed in an occupied latrine.

New Year's came along and we did have a little celebration on New Year's Eve in my platoon headquarters. A group of us got together and somebody had some goodies from home. We shared them and sang "Auld Lang Syne." It was all the more touching because we all realized that some of us were not going to last long into the new year, and in fact, few of those that were there did. One that did, beside myself, was my old buddy whom I called always Sarge. Sarge had a name but I cannot remember it. We got along very well, and although he was a reticent man he was always ready to help me and I him. I think he appreciated the fact that like him I was a survivor and in fact we two managed to be among the very few from our company who survived through the winter and to the end of the War.

Shortly thereafter I had my medic buddy examine my left foot, which was bothering me a great deal. He found out that I had a bad case of trench foot in both feet and I was sent to a hospital in Belgium. When I got there I had other complaints, too, and the doctors said, "Well, we'll give you an exam. Strip." So I started stripping. At that time my upper body was covered by eight layers of clothing. After I'd removed about six of them one of the doctors said, "For God's sake soldier, is there any of you under there?" There was not much. I had gotten down to a hundred and eighteen pounds. They put me in a bed with my feet elevated, one of a long line of soldiers with trench foot, which was prevalent as a result of the winter operations and our inadequate footwear. The regulation Army boot was not fit for winter use at all. It was leather and when it got soaked with water it became stiff. If you took it off it froze and you couldn't get it on again. It was just a nuisance. Shortly thereafter they issued a much more practical winter boot, styled after the L.L. Bean hunting boot, with rubber bottoms and leather tops, a great improvement that led right away to the diminution of trench foot. In addition to the trench foot – which left me with an opening down the bottom of my left foot that went almost to the bone the full length of the foot and a lesser one on the right foot – I had frostbite in both big toes, the left one much worse than the right.

We were laid out, with our feet coated with benzoin, with which I was familiar, having used it on the runners' feet when I was a track manager in college. The result was about a ten-day rest. I spent it sleeping, reading from the extensive library of paperbacks the hospital had, and talking with buddies there. That rest came not a moment too soon and it was so beneficial, I think it probably enabled me to survive the following months. I gained some weight. We were fed well, with hot food every day. When I was able to go back to the company, I found them getting ready to launch into the next stage of operations, the German breakthrough having collapsed.

VII

On to the Rhine

When I got back to my outfit I found that I had been replaced as a runner, so I went back into battle as a regular rifleman right in the middle of a firefight that went on for a day or two. As we were approaching the Roer River dams again, my particular outfit was aimed at Dam #3. The Germans blew up a piece of that dam producing high waters down below, but eventually we drove them out and they withdrew to the eastward. During that engagement the boy who had succeeded me as runner became a casualty so after a couple of days I stepped back into my old job.

I think it was about this time that they began using artificial moonlight a good deal. It was a technique whereby the overhanging clouds, of which we usually had plenty, were illuminated by searchlights, very powerful searchlights. They produced an eerie effect particularly when the searchlights were some distance from our location. This glowing sky would cast a dimly perceptible illumination on the ground, punctuated by all the light effects produced by combat itself.

As a runner I had my choice of what weapon to carry. Initially I preferred to carry the carbine, which was a lighter version of the M-1 rifle. It was usually carried by officers. The regular M-1 was too heavy for me. I got a terrible score in training with it and a much better score with the carbine, which surprised many people. The usual result was the other way around. However, when winter weather overtook us I turned in the carbine and got what we called a grease gun. It was an all-metal, skeleton stock, stubby .45 caliber submachine gun issued to the tankers so they'd have something compact and easy to store. I chose it because it was very simple in its operation and had few moving parts making it easy to keep clean and lubricated in the winter which presented problems for the regular rifles. Ice, mud and slush would get into them and jam them. The grease gun had a very rudimentary sight, but nobody used the sight anyway. You fired it from the hip or from the crook of your arm and just sprayed .45 caliber slugs out in front of you. It was designed primarily for defensive work I think and I only rarely had to use it.

Among our small arms most feared by the Germans, as some of the prisoners told us, was the BAR, the Browning automatic rifle that we inherited from World War I. It was heavy and fussy. It had to be kept very clean and well lubricated, but when it was operating well with a competent operator it was a formidable weapon. It had a little bi-pod at the end of the barrel to rest on the ground on the supposition it would be used from the prone position. However, experienced operators who were physically strong enough preferred to fire it from the hip moving it in an arc and spraying the bullets in front of them.

Our platoon had a BAR man who was particularly good at this. He was a big man, an Indian from Oklahoma. He had long hair and naturally we all called him Chief. I have no idea what his real name was. He never had much to say, but everyone respected his fighting ability. He would stand up and fire the thing from the hip and the Germans would take cover.

One day one of our men was giving him a hard time over something and he didn't say much, but he drew from his boot sheath his infantry knife and, as he had kept the BAR in top condition – oiling and cleaning it whenever he had a little bit of spare time – so also his knife was shining and appeared to be sharp as a razor. He said to the man who was giving him a hard time, "Say buddy, watch this." He pulled one of his own long hairs out until it was taut, just touched it with that knife and it slit it right off as if the knife were a razor. He looked back at the guy and said, "See what I mean?" The guy said, "I get the message, buddy," and he walked off. Unfortunately, the Chief didn't last too long, but while he lasted he was a formidable warrior. I believe he was wounded out. At any rate he never came back to our outfit.

As I have mentioned before, among the weapons the Germans had that gave us a particularly hard time and that we feared the most were the 88 mm cannons. They were adapted to all kinds of mounts, antiaircraft, self-propelled units, and tanks. They fired an 88 mm high velocity projectile and could be fitted with a variety of heads, armor penetrating, explosive and so on. The self-propelled ones were a special hazard. They had a rack that held eight projectiles and they were usually mounted on caterpillar treads, although I saw some on big truck bodies. They'd pull up to a pre-selected location, get off those eight rounds in fairly rapid succession, and then be out of there to a new location before our heavy artillery could spot them.

The other weapon we particularly feared was a little Schmeisser submachine gun we all knew as the burp gun because it fired in bursts of extremely rapid fire, giving a kind of "buurrp" sound. They were deadly because they were high velocity, with a small projectile, and when they penetrated a man's body the little slug would tend to spin around and do a lot of damage. I think that's what got my first lieutenant, Reardon. They also were typical of the German ability to make things from the practical point of view. When the barrels burned out they simply had to be unscrewed, a new barrel screwed in, and they were ready to go again. The rest of them looked like a tinker toy made of pressed metal.

The panzerfaust was another one, an anti-tank weapon, a single shot affair, something like a bazooka. The hollow thin metal tube had at the end of it the explosive head. You fired the head, which was shaped to penetrate armor, although they occasionally used it against other things, any kind of impediment they ran into. Then they just threw away the pipe that was used to fire it. It could do a lot of damage at short range. We had the bazooka that did the same thing. It fired a rocket with an electrical triggering apparatus. There was a hollow tube that fired the rocket out of one end and out of the rear end came the rocket back blast so you had to stay well clear of that.

On one occasion some recruits came in and complained that they had had no training in the bazooka, which was probably true. By 1944 they were sending in young guys with very short training. For some reason I was assigned to instruct them in the bazooka. I had been trained in the bazooka, although I had never used it in combat, so I undertook the instruction. Everything went fine in the erect position, but then I got down into the prone position to demonstrate it. My students were lined up there in a semicircle behind me at a safe distance, they thought. But I, and they, overlooked the fact that right behind me was a large puddle of water and very soft mud. I fired the rocket at the target and the back blast of the rocket picked up a lot of that mud and water and sprayed my students spectacularly. I was relieved of that duty forthwith.

On our side the heavy artillery was one of the weapons most feared by the Germans, as they later told us. We had two heavy artillery pieces that fired from several miles behind the lines. One was the 155 mm long rifle. When the shells went over they sounded like a railroad train going by. They fired over our heads of course. The other was the big 205 mm howitzer. They fired at a high elevation and could be extremely destructive against buildings, tanks and other large targets. The only problem with both of those weapons was that it took them rather a long time to get established and get zeroed in on the enemy. They relied on a spotting plane which we often saw going over our heads. These little planes, like a piper cub, flew at a low elevation and being slow and low were not often attacked by German planes, although there were occasions when they were.

Our tanks were faster than the Germans', but they were more lightly armored and the German heavy tanks were very much superior in that they could outgun our tanks before they could get into effective range. The advantage of our tanks was their maneuverability. Initially ours had 75 mm guns. The Germans had 88 mm guns in many of their tanks that could outrange ours considerably and at higher velocity, which meant they hit harder. Later on the German tanks got even heavier, but they were also slower. The Americans introduced the General Pershing tank that was more a match for the German tanks. It was heavier but it was also faster and was armed with a 90 mm high velocity gun. We had taken the hint from the Germans, and when the Pershing tanks appeared, they were extremely effective.

After we left the Roer dams we headed into the Rhineland. The whole terrain was utterly different. It was open and pretty flat and it extended all the way to the Rhine River, which we and the Germans both understood was a sort of final barrier. If we could pass that we'd win shortly. If the Germans couldn't hold it they were done. Both sides understood this.

The new Rhineland fighting involved largely village fighting. The area was heavily populated with farm villages on large flat expanses, and these villages were little fortresses in themselves because they consisted of a cluster of farms mostly around a central square. The farmyards were walled at the rear, joining each other and presenting a considerable barrier. The farmers lived in the village and went out into the countryside to do their farming. The same thing held even for individual farms. They were built in that same style. This kind of fighting took some getting use to, but once we got used to it we learned to do it quite effectively. The tanks played a big part here because the country was open and they could maneuver and we could follow them. The Germans, however, were in their homeland, the heart of their homeland, and they weren't about to give us an easy time. They defended virtually every village that was in any sense defensible and so we would plod forward following the tanks. We often went into attack following the tanks on foot at night. This too was a new thing, night fighting, which could be carried on in this open countryside. We had some interesting adventures as a result.

In one village we found ourselves there before some of the Germans had left. We were setting up the platoon command post in a big potato cellar when a German patrol surprised us. I think it surprised them too because their reaction was disorganized and hastily they threw hand grenades at us. They were the small goose-egg-size grenades that were more useful for upsetting their victims than wounding them, but at any rate we were in the potato cellar, so we shut the heavy plank door on them. They hurled egg grenades against the door. Fortunately it held, although there was about an inch-and-a-half opening under it and the grenades blasted dust and dirt and a lot of stuff through there. We were ready to fight had they broken in, but they didn't. They took off.

On another occasion there was a big night attack on one of the larger villages. The Germans resisted strenuously and we had brought up the artillery using artificial moonlight. My medic friend and I took cover under a truck and watched it like a Fourth of July show. The projectiles were flying both toward us and away from us, and ours were by far the heavier fire. Fire soon burst out in the town. We used magnesium shells which set fire to anything flammable that they hit and rockets were fired to increase the illumination. Parachute flares of different colors floated through the sky. There were colorful explosive bursts. It was a great show and then when the village was wildly burning we started to surround it, the Germans having finally withdrawn. Few of the attacks were as spectacular as that one. When we took a village we would quite often spend the night there putting up outposts a few yards away from the edge of the village. At dug in positions tanks would serve as strong points at appropriate locations.

One of my functions as runner was to take the current password out to these outposts at twilight. It had to be twilight because by daylight I was too good a target for the snipers and I couldn't go after dark because I couldn't use a light. Thus there was a small time window that I had to do it in. One evening, when I had gotten well out toward the outpost, a figure suddenly came up out of the ground a few yards in from of me. There was enough light left for me to determine instantly that it was a German, from his helmet primarily, and I was lucky in that he had his back to me when he first came out of his hole. I flourished my grease gun and shouted, "Hände hoh!" at him. He responded by dropping his rifle and turning around to face me with his hands up. I don't think my gun was even cocked.

Two or three things went instantly through my mind. One was, if he has any buddies here, I'm a prime target. Two, I've got to get the word out to the outpost. Time is getting shorter by the moment. What am I going to do with him? I took him back to the nearest tank that was dug in. The tank was buttoned up so I banged on the front end of it where the eye slits were. The fellow inside wanted to know what was going on. I told him the situation and he said, "Oh, kill the bastard." And I said, "No no, I have to take him back to the headquarters were they'll interrogate him." They said all right they'd keep him under observation while I went out and did my mission, which I did. Then I came back and got him and took him back to the command post, which was in a cellar or a big foxhole – I forget exactly which.

The boys all laughed at me because there I was, five feet five inches tall and about 118 pounds and my prisoner was over six feet and built like a weightlifter. We had him strip in order to search for hidden weapons. He turned out to be a nineteen-year-old member of the Hitler Jugend and he was indeed a fine physical specimen. One of our sergeants was Jewish and he was our interrogator. In due course the prisoner asked where we were going to send him. We told him England, which was the case. He said, "You can't send me to England. The Führer said that England has been destroyed." We informed him that we had news for him and his Führer, and had him dress. Then I had to escort him at gunpoint back to the company headquarters which was in another part of the town.

While we were on the way some German artillery came in. We both hit the ground and waited and the only thing that came close to us was a dud. Late in the War the Germans were firing a lot of duds. I learned later that slave laborers in the manufacturing plants that were making ammunition were sabotaging a lot of the ammunition. Even though the dud does not explode, it is a frightening object to come sailing in, hitting the ground with a prodigious thump and then going end over end bouncing across the landscape for forty to fifty yards. If that hits a man, he's had it. This one hit pretty close to us with a great thud, close enough to throw dirt on us and we both laid very low. I followed my usual practice of fitting myself into a tank track in the mud. I got him to company headquarters and returned, but the guys never forgot it. They would always joke about Richie's prisoner.

On another occasion we got established in town for the night and then orders came through that we were to move out about 1:00 A.M., so the outpost had to be alerted. One outpost was divided off from us by a minefield. I suppose it was about thirty yards wide. Through it ran a two-inch tape trail. The tape was stapled to the ground in a zigzagged route under heavy trees. It was dark – cloudy with no moon. I had to go out through that minefield following that little tape to the outpost and bring back the three guys who were out there. I got a flashlight that had the lens covered with red plastic with only a little hole about a half an inch in diameter in the middle for the clear white light. Holding that just a few inches from the ground and bent over, I made my way through the minefield along that tape. Needless to say I was sweating a bit by the time I got out there, and then I had to turn around and come back again by the same route.

As we progressed toward the Rhine we got news that a bridge remained over the river. I believe it was the 9th Armored Infantry Division that got there first and went across. We followed on and I think we were the second, the 9th Infantry Division. Our battalion was in the rear on that occasion and some of us were assigned as supply guards because the first thing that occurred was that supplies began piling up at the river. There was only that one route across. It was a railroad bridge just one track wide and something like four hundred yards long, an arch bridge made of iron. I and two other buddies were put on supply detail temporarily at a big farm stand some distance before we got to the Rhine. The standard procedure was two on and one off through the night, spelling each other.

That night one of the boys wasn't feeling well at all, so we agreed that it would be one on and one off and he could sleep the whole time. We were far from the river, and enemy troops were doing their best to get to the other side of the river at that point, so we weren't much concerned. The farm was a big farm then occupied by some Poles who had been slave laborers. The Americans freed them, but they had nowhere to go so they just stayed there because they had food, cows and chickens. We got settled down for the night. We had been observing the first signs of spring.

This was going into March and although the winter had been tough, it faded very quickly after we got out onto the Rhineland plain and began to see little green grass coming up and wheat starting to sprout. This particular night there was quite a strong breeze from the south. I had the 2:00 to 4:00 A.M. shift. I was outside enjoying the feeling of that southern wind, a warm wind for a change. It was thrilling to feel it. I was overcome by the sensation of the arrival of spring. I stripped off my clothes and stood naked in the night enjoying the tremendous feeling of energy that seemed to pour into me from the earth and the sky. The sky was clear. The stars were brilliant and the earth emanated a fertile scent under the stimulus of that warm southern wind. I suddenly felt that things were going to go all right for the first time since I got into combat. I felt optimistic and energy seemed to fill me from my feet to my head, all around. After that I dressed and enjoyed the rest of my spell during the night. I had experienced a kind of pagan epiphany, getting from the earth the energy and hope and belief that I was going to live through it all.

The next morning turned out to be a beautiful day, the warm weather persisting. The first thing I noticed was that

I was very hungry and then I heard the chickens. Now, I hadn't had a fresh egg since I left the United States and I began to have visions of scrambled eggs – fresh scrambled eggs. Curiously, my buddies didn't seem particularly interested, so I went off on my own into the farm and found that the Polish workers had not moved into the main part of the farmhouse but were still in their regular quarters. The Germans had fled or deserted the place and left everything as it was, undamaged. Having no farm background I didn't realize how ferociously a hen would defend her eggs. However, although I was wounded a bit in the hands by this wild hen (my only wounds from a German source) I got two eggs. The chickens had been liberated or had gotten away and were nesting on their own wherever they found a partly hidden place on the farm, and when I got two eggs out from under that hen she was furious. I did get them, however, and then I needed some milk to make scrambled eggs. I noticed that the Poles were milking the cows, so I took my GI cup and some cigarettes and approached one of the milkers indicating by sign language my desire for milk. Flourishing the cigarettes I quickly had a cup of milk. I went back, found a big skillet and made up a fire in the stove with the ever-present coal briquets, which burned hot and cleanly as always, and soon had myself a big pan of scrambled eggs. I must say they were the best tasting scrambled eggs I've ever had.

Shortly the supplies were picked up by a truck and we were taken back to our outfits. I went across the Remagen bridge on a jeep. The method was that we would be lined up behind sheltering buildings and then one by one the vehicles would go over, making a wild dash across the bridge which was under German fire. The Germans tried every conceivable way to blast that bridge. Their initial explosions were all set, but we came more quickly then they anticipated and they didn't succeed in setting most of them off. The few they did set off created damage, but we were able to repair that. Then they fired from a distance. Heavy artillery, rockets, and planes with a single bomb trying to bomb it. This went on for the whole six days before the bridge finally did collapse. I went across probably about the third day on the jeep. The Germans themselves had laid planks on the railroad so that regular vehicles could go over readily, but it was a very rough ride and we were under artillery fire. However, I arrived where we had established a headquarters on the east bank of the river near two or three small towns. We entered the town of Linz and there set up a defense perimeter because the Germans were continuously attacking. The railroad on the eastern side plunged into a tunnel under a very large hill there. The hill was under German control, but the tunnel furnished shelter and we were able to drive the Germans out at the other end.

We were taking heavy casualties. Fighting was intense because the Germans wanted to drive us back into the Rhine. An offensive was planned by all of the outfits there in different directions. We were on the right of the eastern end of the bridge – which was the southern side – and it looked as if it was going to be really bad. Word came down from supply that they needed more men to help with supplies. They were piling up on the western end of the bridge in the town of Remagen to a tremendous extent. My lieutenant said, "Richie, you've been around here a long time, you go over for a while and work with supply." I didn't hesitate. I got a ride back across the bridge to the other side and went to work for supply. I was also fighting a little battle of my own with a bad case of diarrhea, but one of my medic friends loaded me with paregoric and bismuth and that pretty well took care of the situation.

We were up on a high hill, virtually a mountain on the west side that overlooked the bridge at some distance, with a bird's-eye view of the fights that went on in the vicinity of the bridge. The one that was the most spectacular was an air fight between the first German jet that I ever saw (they got them into battle near the end of the War) and a P38, which I believe was our fastest and most maneuverable fighter plane at the time. That was the model with the double tail. They ran down the river, the jet pursuing the P38. The P38 outmaneuvered the jet and they came back up the river in a wild scramble. They were at a very low elevation, almost as low as we were over on that big hill. The jet was faster than the P38 but the P38 could outmaneuver it. We watched with fascination as the jet exploded in midair when shots from the P38 nailed it, but the P38 itself was hit and went down into the river. The pilot was able to parachute out, his parachute opening just barely before he hit the ground, and he was rescued. He landed on our side of the river, but the jet pilot must have died in his plane because the thing disintegrated with a tremendous explosion and the wreckage went into the river.

Meanwhile our troops were laying pontoon bridges across the river, downstream from the Remagen bridge. Ultimately, we had four or more, I can't remember exactly, but we had several, I remember that. And of course they were all under fire so they were having a rough time. The Army engineers were working furiously there and they were also working

The author on a high hill on the west side of the Rhine overlooking the town of Remagen. Beyond his helmet is the Remagen Bridge, the scene of the first Army crossing. The bridge was destroyed by the Germans within a few days of this picture in an attempt to slow down the advances of the Allies.

furiously on the Remagen bridge which had to be constantly repaired as shots hit it every day. Many artillery shots hit it and it was looking more shaky all the time. A unit of the Navy brought boats over land to help provide transportation by boat across the river. They were more efficient boats than we had and there was a lot of joshing of the Army by the Navy boys. They said, "Oh well, you Army people, we have to come to your rescue when things get really tough," and all that sort of thing.

Once, while we were sitting up on that hill having a lunch break, there were three of us in the room of an old building and a flight of rockets came in from the German side, producing a hideous explosion after their shrieking descent. The Germans liked to put those screamers on rockets because they had a psychological effect. The things exploded right outside the building, blew all the windows in on that side and the concussion was such that I ended up over in a corner against the far wall, but unhurt. The other fellows in the room were also essentially unhurt, although a couple had cuts from broken window glass. That sort of thing was part of the daily routine. We didn't think too much about it. The old saying "a miss is as good as a mile" was part of our regular thought.

I was over on the east side of the river toward the end of that week in a big building we had occupied as both kitchen and supply building. I learned that my company was among those out on attack, but they were in trouble so we waited nervously to see what the reports would be. Night came on and men began filtering back. It seems they'd run into real trouble with the Germans and the commander had given the order, "Every man for himself, get back during the night to the river if you can." Quite a few of the men did and we waited for them to come in, but there were heavy losses.

The events weren't all tragic, however. In the basement of this building we discovered an area that had been bricked up, obviously freshly done. That could mean two or three things, but the thing we thought it meant was that it was the wine cellar. The question was how to get it broken open without breaking the wine bottles. The head cook allowed that he could do it, he thought. He worked very skillfully and used bread dough to pack his explosive, which he got by using powder from hand grenades. It worked perfectly. He made a workable hole in the new brickwork and not a bottle was broken. One of the guys asked him, "Hey Cookie, where did you learn to do that?" And Cookie said, "You don't ask me that question, buddy." We made good use of the wine. There was a huge wine warehouse nearby and that was put under guard. But even under guard somebody succeeded in breaking in and making off with a considerable amount of the wine.

I was never a heavy drinker, still I enjoyed wine now and then and under the severe conditions of military life I drank more than I ever did at any other time in my life. I formed a taste for Rhine wine, a white wine that is rather tart and very refreshing.

The Germans had not warned the civilians that we were so close, and when we got word that the bridge was available all troops were ordered to head for that bridge. All up and down the river the outfits that we had there headed for that Remagen bridge crossing. The civilians were still there in Linz and in other villages along the Rhine and were pretty much taken by surprise. Some of them committed suicide and some of them hid out. Some showed signs of great terror, which is hardly surprising because the amount of shells and ammunition that was coming in from both sides was tremendous. A lot of people fled. Where they fled to I never found out. That was true all along the way.

Six days after the crossing the Remagen bridge collapsed. I was over on the east side when it happened and there was no warning. Even at some distance away, we heard this terrifying shrieking sound of rending steel and a number of the engineers who were on it at the time were killed. Others were injured and a big operation was immediately set up to rescue those who were caught in the wreckage. Thereafter the pontoon bridges and the Navy's boats had to serve.

Having crossed the Rhine and set up bridgeheads, all units were having great difficulty breaking out to the eastward. The Germans were staging a desperate defense. At that point a young major took over command of our battalion. I was still in supply, which had by then moved its principal operation to the east side of the Rhine also. The major, new to battle, ordered my company into attack, specifying the objective. My company commander objected strenuously. He was a veteran combat commander, up for the third time after being twice wounded. He sensed a trap, and refused to lead his men into the action the major ordered. The major then relieved him and ordered him court martialed.

A new captain came to take command and the major, to show how wrong the former captain had been, stated he would lead the battalion headquarters right along with company headquarters. Normally battalion HQ would be well in the rear. This plan was carried out and the Germans captured the whole outfit, battalion headquarters, company headquarters, the major, the captain and most of the men. Fortunately, within a week the rest of our division broke out to the east, recaptured our men – who had been imprisoned in a stockade not far to the German rear – and captured a lot of the Germans too. The major was forthwith retired from combat duty. Whether the court martial of our former captain was ever carried out I never learned. Supply sat on the Rhine through all this, anxiously awaiting news. After our men were recaptured and the company reformed, I rejoined it again as runner. Incidentally, the time I was assigned to supply was the first opportunity I had to sleep in a bed since I had gotten to Europe. We had only cots in the hospital. It was a big German featherbed and I reveled in it.

Still near the Rhine, about this time I decided I should have a pair of binoculars in this wide open country. Doing my running and other things, I could use them. I spoke to my old buddy, the sergeant, who was out on a combat patrol in which prisoners were brought in, among them a German artillery-spotting officer. He would not need his binoculars any longer so the sergeant took them and gave them to me. I still have them. They are first-rate Leitz binoculars.

Later on I smashed my wristwatch and suggested to Sarge that I could use a watch. He brought me back a pocket watch – a silver pocket watch with gold hands, apparently of local manufacture. The Germans had watchmakers in some of their towns. I never learned where Sarge got it from, a living soldier or a dead one. I suspect the latter. At any rate, it served me all through the rest of the War and until I got home. Shortly after I got home it stopped and never ran again.

VIII

The Final Push

After leaving the Rhine and breaking out of that region – which involved some very heavy fighting – we headed for the Ruhr Pocket. We were on the southern side of it. A huge pincer movement was exercised on the Ruhr, which was a principal manufacturing area of the Germans. There was a good deal of sharp fighting and a repetition of the village fighting on a larger scale. It was in this area that we had some cities and great factories to contend with. I don't remember that I had any very frightening experiences there, just the usual routine of ducking from cover to cover, trying to shoot and avoid being shot at. I had a lot of running to do I know and there was such rapid change in officers that I didn't get very familiar with any of them.

I carried on a custom I had started when I first became a runner. I helped in the distribution of rations and I always found out what rations were my lieutenant's favorites and made sure that he got some of those. I helped with the distribution of mail and on those occasions when I got a box of things from home I would distribute most of them among my buddies. That was a practical as well as friendly gesture because I couldn't carry very much. As did all the older veterans, I stripped my things to a minimum so that I had a small backpack and that was it. I depended a good deal on finding things I needed as I went along. I also found some of the supplies in wrecked German houses welcome.

In particular I remember a lieutenant who loved a kind of little Portuguese canned oysters. They were very good and a lot of German houses had them. Apparently Germany was able to get supplies from Portugal, which was neutral during the War. I kept busy that way when I was not actually doing my duties, carrying messages and things of that sort. Whatever no one was specifically assigned to do I took on. It kept me busy and occupied. It got me around so that most of the men got to know me and I got to know them, however briefly. The turnover was so great that I never got to know anybody very well, except for Sarge who stayed with us until the end of the War. Occasionally I would see others I knew when I would get to the company headquarters. I saw Jack, the radio man, who also managed to survive to the end. I hardly had a chance to get to know anybody else very well. Jack also cued me in on the latest rumors. A runner's duties were only vaguely specified, and I had from the start determined to make the most of the job. Most of my lieutenants approved.

On one occasion I caused a little stir. A small factory, which was out in the countryside, had been used to manufacture artificial rubber, which was one thing the Germans were still producing. I don't know how it was done but I know that at one point the product was a tar-like liquid. I had a few minutes of exploration in that little factory and I pulled a release lever which opened a flow of the tar-like liquid out onto the floor. A huge quantity of it came pouring out. I was unable to close the valve. I escaped from the building, but the stuff poured out like something in a comic movie. It poured out endlessly from openings in the building and thus I took part in the sabotaging of a Nazi factory.

The Final Push

After getting out of the Ruhr Pocket we headed for the Hartz Mountains where it was reported that Nazi gangs and gangs of Hitler Jugend had holed up and were planning guerrilla warfare against our troops. The Hartz Mountains reminded me a good deal of the Maine mountains, so I felt sort of at home. The first blush of spring was coming on full tilt by that time. It was well into April.

Also at that time, having lost our company commander there near the Rhine we got a new one. He was by far the best combat officer I had in the Army. We called him Captain K. He should have been a lot more than a captain, but he was outspoken in his opinions, particularly his opinions of some of his higher officers, and that doesn't get you promotions in the Army. So he was still a captain and company commander and he didn't care because his chief concern at that point was to get back to civilian life. I liked him at once and apparently it was mutual.

When he first came on board he summoned all the platoon lieutenants with their sergeants and runners to a conference out in the open air. It was on a hilltop near the edge of woods and not far away there was actual combat going on, near enough so we could hear it and see the dust rising. So the conference was kept short. He gave his instructions with great brevity and conciseness and then he said, "Who's the senior runner here?" Sarge stepped forward and said, "Richie here's been here since Bull Run." The captain looked at me and said, "Soldier, when did you come on line?" I said, "'Bout the end of last September." And he said, "You're still here? You must be a damn fast runner or else you're a damn good liar. Anyway, from now on you're my runner. Get your stuff and join the company headquarters." I didn't have much stuff, but I got it

Blood and Candles

The headquarters staff of Company B, 60th Infantry Regiment of the 9th Infantry Division. The author is sitting on the jeep bumper at the right. Captain K, the company commander, is standing at the left. This photo was taken in the Hartz Mountains during a sweep to flush out groups of SS and Hitler Youth who were fighting guerrilla style even after it became apparent that the War was nearly over. Many of the regular German Army troops had already surrendered to the Americans to avoid having to surrender to the Russians.

The Final Push

and joined the headquarters. Like the other veterans I had slimmed down the amount of stuff I carried as I went along and ended up with only the very minimum necessities.

When we moved into the Hartz Mountains – as I said, very much like the Maine mountains: wooded, rolling, but not really very rugged – we were confronted with small groups of the Hitler Jugend, usually under command of an SS man. They were fighting guerrilla warfare at that point. One day Captain K was with most of the company on a mission some distance out in the woods, and we at headquarters were left dug in along a hardwood ridge. We were surprised there by a group of the Hitler Jugend, who attacked from two or three angles using panzerfausts and small arms fire. We returned the fire and thought we had driven them off. The boy next to me got out of his hole to get on his knees to pee. He was promptly shot through the head. He had never learned, unfortunately, a lesson that I had learned in my boyhood when I was playing cowboys and Indians (I was usually an Indian), and that was learning to pee in the prone position without getting myself wet.

After the Hitler Jugend pulled out, we decided that they would probably hit again. We thought there were more than I guess there actually were, and we took off down the slope in the direction the captain had gone. We soon met him coming back with the rest of the troops and he said, "Where are you guys heading? What's going on?" We told him and I said, "Captain, we are making a strategic withdrawal," echoing the official Army rule that the American Army never retreats. He said, "Well, I can see the withdrawal all right, but just turn around, we're going back." So we did.

On another occasion we were joined by tanks and we were going to make a long downhill run toward a town still occupied by the enemy. After an initial exchange of fire for a few minutes, we started a charge down the hill, the tanks moving fast. We were riding on top of the tanks. It felt somewhat as it must have felt in the old days when participating in a horse cavalry charge. It went well and we could see the German troops pulling out at the other end of town as we came down the hill. As they pulled out of the town, the civilians hung out sheets and other white cloths to indicate their surrender. It was a pretty wild day all in all.

This is a time to look back a little bit in my story to when we had just passed over the Roer River and were still in the mountainous wooded areas. We were about to set off on an attack on high ground one morning when we were fired on by a self-propelled 88 and smaller arms. Having fought that off, we started off on the attack, the first platoon on the right, second platoon on their left. We were supposed to go side by side, but soon we discovered that we'd lost contact with the second platoon and the lieutenant figured that we had gone astray somewhere. He had a rudimentary map which he went over with me. He ordered me to go back to find the second platoon and also the company headquarters, to see if we could figure out where we were supposed to be and why we had lost contact. I started out. After awhile I came upon a tote road going up the slope through the woods, which was still pretty much bare of leaves, and I decided I'd better take a compass reading. However, in doing so I made a fundamental error. I was pretty nervous, I guess. I was out there alone in the woods and it seemed to be much too quiet. I failed to take my helmet off when I read the compass and the steel helmet threw the compass off. As a result, I turned right when I should have turned left.

I proceeded along the trail a little way and came to quite a wet, muddy spot. I noticed all the footprints were going the same way I was and that they were the footprints of hobnail boots, which meant Germans. They were the only ones who wore hobnail boots. I immediately perceived that something had gone wrong and, thinking back on my actions, I realized I had misread the compass, so I read it right this time and found I was going the wrong way. Then, looking through the trees, I could see a sharp height of land not far away and I got the idea of going up there to see if I could see anything that would indicate where I might be going. When I got there, I saw the prints and the debris that indicated that that had been the spot from which the self-propelled gun had been firing at us that morning. That made me even more nervous. That gun had been pulled out surely, but were there any German troops still around? I didn't know. It was very quiet, but that only made the situation seem more ominous. I laid out a course and started back down toward what I conceived to be the advance of our own troops.

Then the thought struck me, how am I going to get back into my own lines? I'm out here in no-man's land. And then again my experience as a boyhood Indian came back to me. I got off the pathway and skirted through the woods parallel to it, being quiet, stopping often to listen, and soon, sure enough, I heard the advance of the American troops, who were notoriously noisy when they thought no enemy was around. I hid in the woods behind a fallen tree and let the point pass. Pretty soon a sergeant came up with more troops. At some point I was going to have to reveal myself and this seemed to be the right time. I called out without showing myself. I called out to the sergeant and said, "Hey, Sarge, a lost GI in here, can I come out?" Everyone went into alert position ready to fire and he said, "Yes, come out with your hands up, whoever you are." I put my weapon on the fallen tree and went out with my hands up. Captured by my own troops. What an embarrassment. It was more than an embarrassment; it was a very dangerous situation.

Earlier on, during the breakthrough, the Germans had parachuted many of their own soldiers behind our lines dressed in American uniforms, and they were such a menace that we had orders at that time to shoot them on sight. Sure enough, the tough little guy beside the sergeant said, "This guy has to be a Kraut. We should shoot him." The sergeant calmed him down and began asking me questions. Right out of the movies, he asked me questions about professional baseball players and baseball teams, one subject about which I knew nothing. I never cared for nor took any interest in baseball, so I told him so and that didn't help at all. The little guy said, "I told you so Sarge, this guy's a Kraut. We gotta kill him." And some of the others looked rather menacing too.

At that point, however, I got a lucky break. The lieutenant of the platoon came along with the rest of the troops and he wanted to know what was going on. The sergeant told him and he turned to me and said, "Where are you from, soldier, back in the States? Where's your home?" I said, "South Portland, Maine." And he said, "Ah, Maine. All right. Tell me the name of the river between Biddeford and its sister city." I said, "It's the Saco River." He said, "Tell me the name of the college that's in Brunswick, Maine." I said, "Bowdoin, that's my alma mater." He asked me a few more questions. He said, "What's the river that runs through Brunswick?" I said, "The Androscoggin." Then he turned to the sergeant and said, "This guy's all right. You can relax." I said to him then, "Sir, are you from Maine?" and he said, "No, I'm from Massachusetts, but during my childhood my folks had a summer cottage in Ogunquit. And I know nobody outside of Maine who hasn't been there a long time who can ever say either Saco or Bowdoin correctly." Then he sent me on my way to company headquarters which was not far behind. That got straightened out, but for a little while I was afraid that I was about to be shot by my own men. It wasn't a pleasant feeling.

One of the places we came to as we were heading toward the Hartz Mountains was Nordhausen. We smelled it long before we got there. Nordhausen was a camp for Polish slave laborers. They were kept there, they were starved, they were mistreated and they died, or they were killed. It was a mess. There were unburied bodies. It was not by far one of the real death camps, but it was close enough to them to give you a good idea of what they were all about. We didn't spend much time there and could only look through the gates at what was inside. Then we passed on.

After we finished at the Hartz Mountains area and got it cleared we went on to the industrial city of Bitterfeld, not far from Leipzig. It had been bombed unmercifully. It was a total wreck, but we moved into a building that was only half destroyed and nearby were the bombed out ruins of an Agfa film factory with photographic material strewn all over.

The author's former platoon at Bitterfeld just before VE Day. The author was no longer a member of the platoon because he was serving as a runner or scout for the company commander, providing a communications link between company headquarters and the platoon.

The Final Push

Nearby was a large retail photo store, also smashed with the contents strewn around. We would have to sit in Bitterfeld for a week or so waiting for contact to be made with the Russians. Having nothing special to do, except ordinary sentry duty and the like, the men picked up cameras right and left and began taking pictures of everything, including each other.

Captain K, knowing my interest in photography and that I was already taking photographs with my own little camera, ordered me to set up a darkroom, get volunteers to assist me and to process the film that the guys were turning out. We took over a machine shop that could be blacked out easily. It still had available running water. I don't know how that worked, but we had running water and we set up developing tanks in the form of ten gallon milk cans, or their equivalent in liters, and processed films for about five days, all day every day. The results were variable in the extreme. We got films that had nothing on them, clear plastic, and others that were coal black with everything in between. The men never knew what kind of film they were getting hold of and they didn't know how to expose it when they got it, so there were numerous problems. Now and then out of sheer luck somebody got a useable photograph. It was great fun, though, and relaxing after what we had been through, so we sat there and enjoyed the hot meals that were provided and relaxed. Something equivalent to a rest club was set up.

I was able to get in a little reading. When I said earlier that I'd stripped what I had to carry to the minimum, there were two exceptions to that. I carried with me all the way through my service, and I still have them, two small books. One was a paperback – a pocketbook of verse, *Great English and American*

Poems. The other was a little hardbound volume, a Modern Library book called *Modern American Poetry.* I enjoyed reading poetry, having been a student of poetry anyway, and poetry was something you could read in bits and pieces as you had a little time to do it.

Looking into these books, I notice that I underlined here and there sections that appealed to me. One that obviously did was Matthew Arnold's "Dover Beach." The last lines applied perfectly to my military experience. "We were here as on the darkling plain, swept with confused alarms of struggle and flight where ignorant armies clash by night." For some reason, at that time Vachel Lindsey's "The Chinese Nightingale" appealed to me a lot. I think it was the general mood of that poem that did it.

I came across other poems that have always stayed with me. Some of my favorites are by Wilfred Owen, the young English poet who was killed in the First World War and who to my mind is the truest of all war poets. I have always left the patriotic rhetoric for politicians' Fourth of July speeches. That sort of poetry has no appeal to me at all.

This was late April. Unofficially the War was over. Officially it was not. We moved out of Bitterfeld after contact with the Russians had been made – not by my particular company, I might add – and settled down in a small town somewhat back to the south. I don't remember its name. We settled into the town hall and established our headquarters there. Right next door was battalion headquarters. We lesser members of the headquarters, Jack and I and others, established ourselves in the jail, which was on the basement floor of the town hall. It made comfortable quarters and was quite warm on the cool nights. The days then were beautiful, beautiful spring weather and everyone was cheerful for a change because of the knowledge that the War would soon be officially over. Nevertheless we were very much on alert because the rumor was that the Germans had established some picked bands of SS and Hitler Jugend in the Alps – the Austrian Alps – which would pour forth and attack us unexpectedly at some point. This later proved to be untrue, but nevertheless, at the time I speak of we didn't know that and so we were very much on alert. Among other things the switchboard, which had connections now with all of our units, had what we called the redline, which ran directly back through regiment and corps and Army to SHAEF, the commanding officer's headquarters in Paris – Eisenhower that is. That was reserved for a crisis if the Germans actually produced a new attack.

I was in charge of quarters one night on the 2:00–4:00 A.M. shift. I was very blurry about 3:00 or 3:30 when I had to ring in to Battalion – as I had to do every half hour – that all was well. Half asleep I fumbled around at the switchboard and, yes, I rang in on the redline. All hell broke loose. Regiment called, battalion called, corps called. I didn't know what to do so I rushed to the captain's quarters and waked him and told him what I had done. He didn't say a word. He rushed down to the switchboard and went to work on canceling the whole operation, which he succeeded in doing after an hour or so of explaining, or trying to explain, to everybody all the way up to SHAEF what had happened. He told me, "Richie, as soon as you have had breakfast in the morning, I order you to disappear. There's a group of inspecting officers coming here from regiment and maybe from even higher and

I don't want you anywhere around, understand?" I said, "Yes sir."

In the morning I took some refreshments and a book and vanished into the old bomb shelter that was opposite the entrance to the town hall. From there I could see the town hall entrance. Sure enough the inspecting crew arrived, three or four vehicles of them, and I guess from what I was told by the sergeant major later, they gave Captain K a very hard time, but he didn't show any particular upset over this. At that point he wouldn't have cared whether he was out of the Army or not, I guess. In any case, they asked what kind of discipline he was exercising on me and I was later told that he said, "Oh, I've put him out to hard labor out in the outskirts of our area." They accepted that and finally went off. After they had gone, I came back and the captain didn't say much of anything to me about it. The sergeant major filled me in on what had happened and remarked that I was a very lucky fellow. In ordinary circumstances, if it had been someone other than Captain K, I probably would have been court martialed even though the whole thing was a mistake.

Later on, we got a new executive officer in the outfit and he was familiarizing himself with the company. He asked Captain K, "What does Richie do around here?" Captain K said, "Oh Richie, I just keep him around for laughs." That sort of represented part of the relationship we had, I guess.

Among the people from battalion who were sharing our quarters in the basement of the building at that time was Jimmy. Jimmy was a young fellow, 19 years old, a wire man, and he was wearing a Bronze Star with Cluster and Purple Heart. I got acquainted with him right away. I liked him very much. He was very obviously gay and I inquired from some of the other wire men how he had come by the decorations and the story was this. Jimmy had run away from home in the deep south in his early teens and gone to New York to become a professional dancer. He was about six feet tall, lean and muscular and had been I think a very good dancer, since I saw him dance later. He had been with two others of the wire team earlier on when they had been ambushed by a German combat patrol with machine guns and burp guns. They knocked down the other two wire men while Jimmy was back at the truck. The two wire men were in bad shape from their wounds. Jimmy, braving the machine gun fire, went out into the open area where they were, rescued one of them using the prone carry technique, which is very difficult and requires a very strong man to do it. I know in the training I had found I simply couldn't do it with a man of average weight and size. While carrying that man in, Jimmy was wounded. However, he went back out and got the second man and he was wounded a second time doing that. Nevertheless, he brought them both in and got them back to the medics. His wounds were not serious; the other men's were serious, but not fatal. Jimmy was considered rather a hero by the other men and very highly regarded, which tends to refute in my mind the present official position of the Army on gay personnel.

Another fellow in the outfit I particularly liked was a boy barely eighteen. In fact, I think he may not actually have been eighteen, but he had just arrived on the front near the end of the War and seen a small amount of action. He was from the Kentucky region I think, and he was not very literate. He was a husky young fellow and he felt that having come and fought at the end of the War, and the War now being essentially over, he ought to be able to go home. To his way of thinking, he'd done his job and that was that. The captain tried to explain to him that that wasn't quite how things worked, but he was stubborn and didn't see it that way and he got put on permanent cleanup detail, cleaning up the latrines, the showers and the like. I had befriended him and the captain noticed this; he detailed me to try to explain to him how the Army worked and why he wasn't going to go home right off. I undertook to try to do that, and over a period of time I think I succeeded, because he got back on regular duty and seemed to be fairly cheerful.

Then the word came down from on high that having nothing much to do, the men should be encouraged to seek wholesome entertainment, playing games and sports and things of that sort, and they approved an idea that Jimmy came up with to produce a musical. He found that several of the men could play musical instruments. They procured some German instruments and Jimmy rehearsed them, set the thing up and designed the whole show like a Broadway musical. He picked a number of the men to play the chorus girls, which was riotous, and he himself was the star and did a tremendous female impersonation. Unfortunately, I didn't get to see the show though I did see the dress rehearsal. I left on pass just before the show was given, but on return I learned that it had been a great success and attended by everybody from the colonel commanding the regiment on down, and they all had greatly enjoyed it.

The pass I speak of came about this way. Captain K said to me one day, "You've been here ever since last fall. Have you ever had a pass?" I said, "No," and he said, "Well it's time you had one. I'm giving you a three-day pass to Paris." So that was what I got. A couple of days later, I headed out by truck to the railhead that the engineers already had established on the German border. They had the trains running from there back into France and I took the train. It was very slow going, because the train had to be sidetracked with some frequency to make room for loads of supplies coming up to the front. Very early the next morning, virtually at the crack of dawn, I awakened. The train had stopped and I heard a great deal of noise outside. We were at the town of Soissons on the French border. The crowd outside was mostly civilian, rapidly joined by GIs from the train, and the shouting was that the War was over officially, and here we were on the way to Paris.

While traveling to Paris on leave, the author took this picture at the exact moment that the news of the official end of the War was released.

IX

VE Day in Paris

The French decorated the front of the engine with iris – the French Fleur de Lys, their national flower – and then, finally, on we went and arrived at Paris, I think at the Gare du Nord, early in the morning. That was the beginning of the wildest celebration I have ever seen in my life or ever hope to see. I got established in my hotel and then came the question of making contact with the black market in order to dispose of the briefcase full of cigarettes that I had brought with me, which would give me a pocketful of money and then some. The sarge had been to Paris before me and gave me some tips on how to go about doing this. After I got freshened up at my hotel and had some breakfast, I went outside to a sidewalk café and sat down with coffee and put the briefcase in full view on the table and waited. Various people came by and then a teenage boy, probably about fifteen or so, came by and he looked promising because I had already learned that the first people to recover form the shock of war and to establish various working relationships with the GIs were the teenagers, boys and girls both. The girls for sex and the boys mostly for commercial enterprises.

This boy looked different from the street boys that were around. He was well dressed. He had on a nylon purple shirt worn as the young Frenchmen all were wearing them that spring – open in front with the shirttails tied around the waist leaving a bare midriff. Shorts and sandals completed the outfit. He went by, our eyes met and he kept on going after a brief glance, but pretty soon he came back again, came directly at my table and very courteously, and in fairly good English, asked if he might talk to me. I said, "Yes, by all means," and invited him to sit down. It took me back a little because he got right down to business and said, "Do you have anything to sell?" I said, "Well, I might have," and he said, "Well, would you have any jeeps?" I said, "No, no jeeps." "Tires?" "No." "Gasoline?" "No." I think we went through a few more things and finally he got down to cigarettes and I said, "Yes, I have some cigarettes." I patted the briefcase. I had already checked with Sarge on how much I ought to be getting for them and the boy didn't beat around the bush. He made his offer and it was what I had expected, so we went across the street to the little park and sat down there, more or less out of the way, and did our transaction. He had a little backpack that turned out to be full of money – francs – and I sold him the whole briefcase of cigarettes, briefcase and all. That was the way I financed my three-day pass.

Loaded with francs, I set out to see the city, which was in a tremendous uproar. The stores were all mostly closed, kegs of wine were set out on the sidewalks, drinks free for the taking. The streets were full of traffic. All of the vehicular traffic was of the armed services because the Germans had made off with all of the French vehicles of any consequence.

However, one thing I did notice that amused me – the French government had furnished disabled soldiers from World War I with little electric tricycle wheelchairs. These were buzzing around and most of them had three or four people clinging to them. It was rather striking. Many allied soldiers were there, including representatives of the Russians and Americans. Finally I gravitated to that huge square in front of the opera, the Place de l'Opéra, which was jammed with people.

Everyone, it seemed, was trying to get into the square. The flags of all of the allied nations had been hung all around on the façades of the buildings, and on the front of the Opéra there was a huge French flag – the tricolor. Every half hour the opera singers would come out on a balcony on the front of the Opéra and sing with the accompaniment of the National Guard Band the national songs of the allied nations, the national anthems. Half an hour later they'd come out and do it again, and so it went. For the first time in six years the lights were on brilliantly. Everyone was cheering every time a new one would come on. But the thing that stays in my mind most vividly was that right next to me there was a young man, apparently a partially-disabled soldier, and on his shoulders was sitting his little son. He kept calling his son's attention to the flag. He would point at that huge flag of France on the façade of the Opéra and he would say to him, "Regard, regard ton drapeau." He kept repeating that and the little kid would clap his hands and cry out. I found that extremely moving. Everyone's emotions were running high, the excitement was incredible.

I must admit that the rest of the night becomes rather blurry for me. It was filled with all kinds of celebrations. There were street dances. People would grab you and kiss you, both sexes, and American soldiers especially were very, very popular. Wine was free everywhere on the streets. It was just a tremendous emotional orgy. I don't think I got back to my hotel until nearly dawn. The next day I started out after awhile wandering around doing sightseeing, among other things getting out to the Arc de Triomphe, where huge flags of the allies hung under the arch. The flame that burns under the arch had been rekindled and there was a great ceremony. A great deal of uproar continued all that day. Wherever I went there were crowds cheering. There were continuous celebrations. At night there were fireworks.

In the evening I had noticed that the Opéra was advertising a night of ballet. I had been quite a ballet fan earlier on, especially when I was in Boston. I determined I would like to go to that. Of course it was jammed. There were no tickets to be had at the box office, but people were out on the steps of the Opéra hawking tickets. I suppose they were higher than the usual prices, but it didn't matter to me. I was loaded with francs and a middle-aged woman had one, which I bought from her. It was way up in a high balcony – about the sixth tier, I guess – and the program was French ballet. The principal ballet was *Giselle*, but I didn't care what it was. After the several months of combat that I had been through, this was pure fantasyland and I sat there with the tears flowing the whole evening. After that I needed sleep and slept long hours that night and into the next day.

The next day I ventured out again for more explorations. That would be my last full day there. I met a boy who was AWOL from the Army hospital. At the end of the War it was said that there were about ten thousand GIs AWOL in Paris for one reason or another. I think that was probably correct. This boy had been in the Army hospital and in the confusion of things toward the end of the War they had mislaid his records, so they couldn't let him out, although he was all cured. He was in a sort of non-person situation. He had slipped out of the hospital, though, and using his cigarettes and what other things he might have to trade, he had made his way around for a few days. But by the time I met him he was pretty well down on his luck. He was eighteen years old, very personable, seemed to be quite intelligent and we chatted and had a pleasant time. Then as night came on, I gave him some of my remaining cigarettes and he traded these for food. I took him home for the night as he had nowhere to go. I slipped him by the concierge by distracting her long enough for him to get through the hall and up to my room.

We spent a pleasant night together and the next morning I figured out how to get him breakfast. He went with me to the great dining hall, which had been set up by the Army for GIs on pass. That morning, like the last two, was a scene of utter confusion. People were jammed shoulder to shoulder and my ticket had only one space left to punch on it. However, the incoming crowd passed by those already admitted into the dining room, only a rail separating them. I managed to slip through without getting my ticket punched and then passed it to him as he came by the other way and we had breakfast together, both on one ticket.

I had quite a few cigarettes left, which I left with him when I departed that morning. At that time American cigarettes had a trading value of approximately $20.00 for a pack, in 1945 dollars. In other words, if you had a bag of cigarettes you were reasonably rich.

I headed back and got to a distribution center in Belgium, in the city of Verviers. There the transportation office told me that my outfit had moved while I was in Paris. They didn't know where it had moved to yet and so I was to stay there in Verviers until such time as they had located my outfit. I was to report twice a day to that office and have my papers stamped so that I wouldn't be held to be AWOL. That is what I did and I explored Verviers and had a couple of interesting experiences.

I noticed that hanging all around the main square in Verviers were huge portraits of President Roosevelt, who had died in April. I think he had made an even bigger impression in Europe than in America. He was looked upon as a sort of savior of the allied countries there and these huge portraits hung all around. While I was riding on a trolley car one day, an aged woman came up to me and squeezed my arm saying, "Votre Président est mort." Your president is dead. Well, that was true and I think the implications of it just began to sink in when I saw how much it had affected these people in Belgium.

Then a remarkable coincidence occurred. I was shopping for books and I was looking in the show window of a large bookshop in Verviers when someone stepped up beside me and said, "How are ya, Eddie?" It was an old friend of mine from Bowdoin College who had become the roommate of the boy who had been my freshman roommate. His name was John Dick. He had been a French major at Bowdoin and in the Army he had been in the medical corps. We immediately had a reunion. He was a book collector too, and we went into the bookstore together. There was a little old lady waiting on trade and after we had looked through quite a few books, John stepped up to her and asked her if she had anything in the realm of the *érotique*. She smiled and winked at us and led us into a back room where there were shelves of books of erotica. He picked out a couple and I picked out one, *Les Chansons de Bilitis*, poems of an erotic nature featuring women's affection for women. What appealed to me about it were the watercolor illustrations of great delicacy; it's a book which I still have.

We had a pleasant visit there and on about the third day they told me that they had discovered where my outfit had gone, which was a place in Bavaria, the southern part of Germany, the opposite part of the country from where I had left them. They got me a travel order that would permit me to travel on any type of Army transportation that was going in the right direction. I ended up in a truck traveling for a good part of one day. We stopped for the night at an old castle that had been renovated to contemporary use. We slept in the grand ballroom of that place. The German Army had used it. They'd cleaned out the furniture and put down straw in the grand ballroom, but the heroic-size paintings of the former occupants still hung on the walls, men in uniforms of the Kaiser's era and women in ball gowns.

In the morning, before we started out, I went out on a little balcony that overlooked the valley below. The castle was up high on a hill, which was typical, and down below was a valley with a stream. I have no idea where this was. I can't remember if I ever knew the name of it. I was standing there gazing out over the stream. A mist was rising. A ruined bridge was half in the stream. There was no sign of life around the village below. Suddenly I became aware of something I had not experienced for a long time. Silence. When I was in combat I was half aware all the time of the noise. There was always noise, a steady sound of guns, vehicles, tanks, trucks, small arms firing close or far away. Always, there was that noise of war. And suddenly I became conscious that this had ceased, that the landscape was peaceful and that the whole area was silent. I took a photograph of that place, which I still have.

We moved on and finally I found my way to where my outfit had established itself, the town of Wolnzach in Bavaria. This was a small town, but rather pleasant. It had not been damaged by the war, which was true of a great deal of Bavaria, and the place was fragrant. There were fields of hops all around and the fragrance of the hops strung up on poles like climbing string beans was everywhere.

While in Paris I had stopped at a couple of the bookstalls along the Seine and I found a copy in English of Henry Miller's *Tropic of Cancer*. That was a book that was barred from importation into the United States at that time. It was considered too obscene. By present day standards it is very mild, but in those days the standards were more severe. This was a curious volume. It had been printed in Hungary during the Nazi era, but was in English, although with some peculiar typographical errors, and it was most interesting. I read it and took it back with me to the outfit knowing Captain K would like it.

He was a well-educated man and had a literary background. My first day back on duty I put it on his desk. He came in and sat down at his desk. I had a little desk, slightly forward of his and lower down. He looked at the book. I'm sure he recognized what it was and he announced rather loudly, "This book I find on my desk could only have been brought to me by one soldier in this office." He looked pointedly at me. I said, "Yes sir, and I thought it would be of interest to anyone of your literary background," and he said, "Well, it is." Then he stood up and said, "I'm going up to my quarters for a little while. If anything important comes up, let me know." He left the office and went back to his quarters with the book, which he later informed me he had read.

We had an arrangement in that headquarters. The wire men had put in a buzzer leading from my desk. The button was underneath the knee space and the buzzer was in Captain K's quarters. My instructions were that if any inspecting officer showed up unexpectedly, and he was in his quarters, I was to buzz him two short buzzes. If any sudden emergency arose I was to give one long buzz. No emergency arose while we were there, but there were some inspecting officers from time to time, and the buzzer system worked very nicely, especially as Captain K occasionally had a visitor in his quarters. At the end of the War we were under orders not to have any communications with the Germans, no fraternization of any kind. Everyone, both officers and enlisted men, ignored that order so extensively that it was quietly withdrawn a little later.

Looking around the countryside I saw a small farmer at a neighboring house who seemed to have a kind of kitchen garden he was working on. I went over to talk to him. His English was no better than my German and we ended up talking together in French. It turned out that he was a former schoolteacher and a very interesting conversation followed. His comments on the War were gloomy, of course. He could see Germany utterly ruined and that bothered him very badly and I understood that. Yet he seemed to be sympathetic to the idea that the Americans were the ones who had taken charge in his area, as everyone feared the Russians. In fact, in our last days there at Bitterfeld and immediately afterwards we accepted literally hundreds of German prisoners fleeing to surrender to us rather than to the Russians.

We in the infantry had a saying that we had to fight two wars, one with the Germans and the other with the Army. The effort to impose more restrictive regulations on us after the end of the War didn't work well at all. We called it "chicken shit." Combat veterans didn't take very kindly to it. All we wanted was to be sent home, but we knew this was unlikely to happen very soon, and for the time being we were in the Army of occupation in Bavaria and trying to get established there.

There was a period between the official end of the War in Europe, which was the 8th of May, and the middle of June, during which I had the opportunity to do some traveling. I was in the company headquarters and at that time a sergeant and three enlisted men could sign out a jeep and take it on a weekend trip to some designated place.

The most interesting of these trips was one that took me to Hitler's villa in Berchtesgaden, and I have a photograph that I took there, looking out over the Austrian Alps through the bombed-out window opening of his famous big picture window. While we were at Berchtesgaden, we went up and visited the Eagle's Nest, Hitler's mountaintop lodge, which

VE Day in Paris

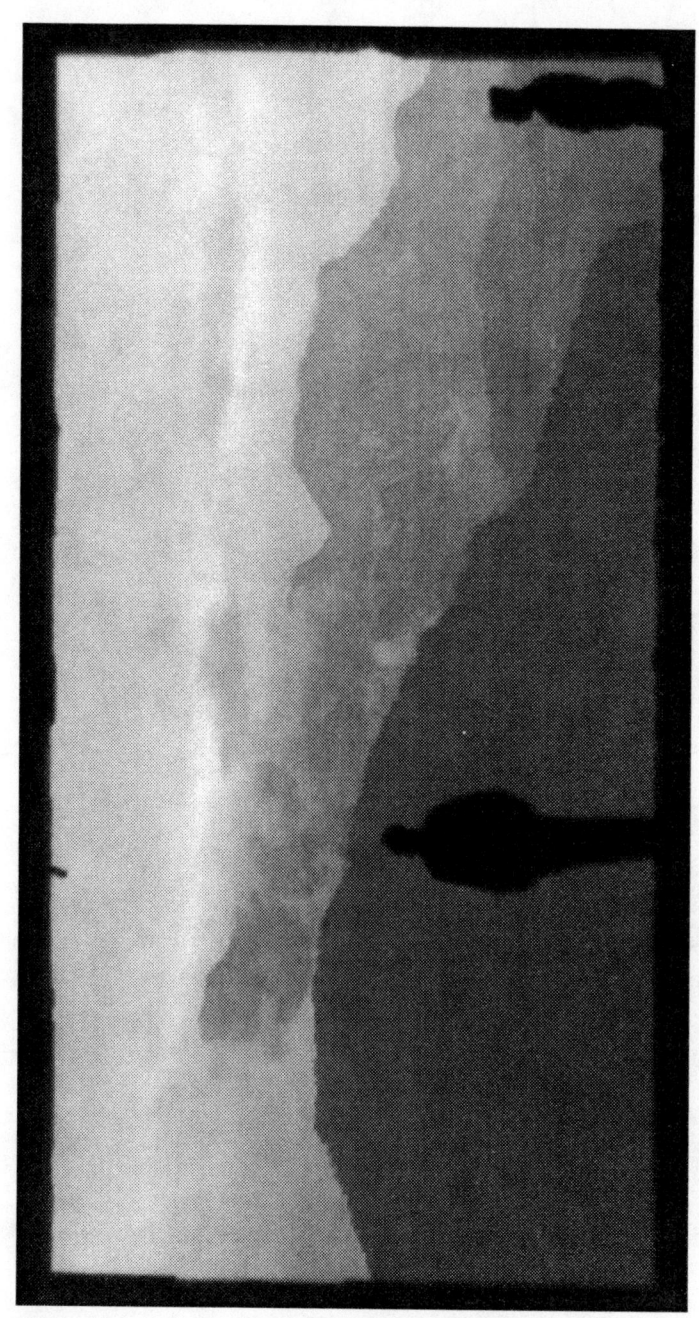

A photo taken by the author of the famous picture window at Berchtesgaden, Hitler's country home, looking out at the Austrian Alps. The glass had been bombed out. The size of the window is shown by the man standing on the window sill.

Hitler's Eagle's Nest, which has been preserved as a tourist attraction.

VE Day in Paris

Interior view of the Eagle's Nest, which was closed shortly after the author's visit because pieces of the carpet and furniture were being taken as souveniers.

The author at the Eagle's Nest, Hitler's private hideaway, at the top of a mountain high above Berchtesgaden.

was intact until soldiers began stealing doorknobs and cutting pieces off the carpets as souvenirs. As a result they stopped permitting us to go up there. I made it up there before that bar was put down and found it intriguing that according to reports, Hitler had spent only three days there in his whole time as dictator. He never had the time, I guess. The villa down below had been bombed out and later on it was bulldozed and completely eradicated. I visited Salzburg also and we took a ride briefly up into the neighboring Alps to look at the scenery.

Later, on another trip, I visited Munich. Munich had been badly bombed and the central part of it – the key buildings, the royal palace, the university, the big state church, and other places of that sort – had been bombed out. That had been the city where Hitler's career originated and the headquarters of the Brown Shirts was there. Then came an unexpected opportunity. I found out that the Army had instituted a program, which was very little known about, to resuscitate the French universities. To qualify we had to make an application on our own initiative, and then submit to an examination. Three of us out of our whole battalion qualified. I was one of them, Jack was another, and the third was from another company in the battalion.

The ruins of a German triumphal arch in Munich.

VE Day in Paris

The great German poet Schiller face down in the dirt.

Fallen statutes in Munich.

VE Day in Paris

Part of the University of Munich just after VE Day.

X

Summer in Paris

In due course late in June we took the train to Paris. The trip from Bavaria to Paris is not really that long. I imagine it would only be a few hours in modern times, but the railroad had just been restored to operations by the American engineers and we had to be sidetracked with great frequency to allow for passing munitions trains. The result was that it took two days and two nights to get there. We three enjoyed the trip in spite of all the delays because Jack and I had already gotten to know each other very well and the third boy turned out to be very compatible. At night we converted that old-fashioned European railway carriage in which the seats pull together and the backs slide down to make a bed that theoretically would hold four people. In fact it was fairly crowded with only three.

We finally made it to Paris and found ourselves taking courses at the Sorbonne – the University of Paris. This was a fascinating experience from many angles. The Army furnished us lodging in a then unused boarding school, a big building, the Ecole St. Louis on the Boulevard St. Michel, which was right around the corner from the University. They fed us with Army rations, but cooked by French chefs in a French restaurant. It is absolutely amazing what those French chefs could do with Army rations. We had gourmet meals. Even Spam could be a tempting dinner under their touch.

Otherwise we were on completely detached service relative to the military. This led to some amusing situations.

One was that, as I said before, Paris was full of AWOL American soldiers and full of military police looking for them. Military police never seemed to understand what our status was. Although we had special ID papers, we were always being stopped and questioned and we got sick of that. We had noticed that returned French soldiers and a lot of young Frenchmen generally, there being a shortage of clothes in France at that time, had gotten hold of used or unused American uniforms, stripped any insignia from them and wore them. They wore them in their own style, that is the shirts open in front, and shirttails tied around the waist. We decided, "Let us become French," since that was the reason we were there, to learn more about the French and French language, and we did. We got some old uniforms from various sources and went out and about that way. If an MP stopped us we would wave our hands and spout at him in French and he would say something like, "Ah, you're only dumb frogs," and he'd pass us on. That worked out pretty well.

One of the first things we needed to do was to establish contact with the black market because Paris, that summer of 1945, was operating entirely on the black market. The franc had been greatly devalued and the Army had pegged its military dollar to support the franc, which meant that we were getting very underpaid if we took cash for our pay. I had arranged that most of my pay went into war bonds automatically, but it didn't matter much because under combat conditions there's nothing you can use money for anyway, except gambling, and I wasn't doing any of that. I forgot how I found her, but I established my contact through a middle-aged lady who kept guard on a public toilet, which was the custom there. They had concierges of the toilet, so to speak, and they were usually widows of war veterans.

She was a large and robust lady and I was told to be sure to tip her well, but what they meant was tip her perhaps three cigarettes. That would be a very generous tip. However, I was a little naive in the matter at that point, and when I went in and established my connection with her, at the end I tipped her with a whole pack of cigarettes. She was delighted and astonished at this. She grabbed me, lifted me off the floor and covered me with kisses, whirling me around. I barely escaped. Thereafter I had no problem whatever whenever I wished to turn my cigarettes into money.

Through a typical Army screw up, I – who never smoked at all – received a double cigarette ration and when I went to Paris I had a whole barracks bag of cigarettes, so I was wealthy. The women in the program, the WACS, the WAVES and the nurses, had a real solution too, whether they had cigarettes or not, because anything in silk or nylon was tremendously valuable, there being not much of either in France at the time. French women were using parachutes to make dresses. Their agent was a young French traffic policeman on the Boulevard St. Michel outside of where we lived. French police wear a cape of waist length, and he showed us one day that he had his cape completely sewed into pockets in the inside. He was the girls' agent for the black market and after he had collected a lot of the lingerie and stockings he looked as if he had gained fifty pounds.

Summer in Paris

The view from the author's dormitory room in Paris, looking down rue de M. le Prince in the summer of 1945.

We went on in this program and got ourselves well-established. The courses were not difficult. They had courses in French language, history, cultural history, political history, art, and music. We were encouraged to use our spare time – and we had quite a lot of it – to go around and explore on our own, and we did.

Six of us who were music lovers had a box for three nights a week at the opera. I forget how many cigarettes this cost us, but not as many as you would think. In dollars I imagine it was several hundreds of dollars, but it didn't matter to us at that point and we saw a great deal of the repertory which alternated between opera and ballet. The ballet was my favorite and the opera was French and Italian opera, but no Wagner. They'd had their fill of Wagner during the German occupation. There were three symphony orchestras functioning in Paris at that time and we covered all three of them. There was also a modern ballet group and we often went to see them. Roland Petit, who later became famous, was just getting started.

The others in our group were very interesting people. All of them had quite rich academic backgrounds. On one occasion, out of curiosity, we decided to check into the activities of the Communist Party there. The communists had been very active in the resistance and were a major force in the political situation in France at that time. We found that there was a communist cell headquarters right next to the university in a little café there, and the six of us went over one night. One member of our group had actually been a member of the Communist Party in New York and he was spokesman. The rest of us kept pretty quiet when we went in. He got us by the fellow at the entrance who was screening people coming in and we got into conversation with two or three of the men there. One of them asked me where I was from and I said, "Maine." He said, "Maine, like Maine in France?" which he knew. He didn't know where Maine was in the United States, but I pointed it out to him on a map that they had there, and he said, "What's the state of the party in Maine?" I said, "Well, I'm afraid there isn't much to hope for in Maine. They're pretty backward politically in that respect." He commiserated with me and said, "Well, do the best you can," apparently assuming I was an organizer or something. After things began to get a little too thick, we left and wrote it down as part of our education.

By that summer the French railways were already operating and they had very fast electric trains leaving from Paris. Jack and I went on several expeditions out into the countryside, and often at some distance from Paris. On one occasion we visited Chartres and examined the cathedral and other things there. On another occasion we took one of the trains and just got off arbitrarily at a little town that was one of the stops. It was a Sunday and very quiet – the silence after the War – and there was an old man fishing in a brook, sitting on a little bridge that crossed it. It was a very rural spot. It was a hot day. We walked down the stream and found a large pool. We took off our clothes and bathed in the pool and then lay in the sun afterwards, sunbathing for awhile. The quiet, the pastoral nature of the whole place, all seemed so incredibly peaceful after what we'd been through. We made other trips of a similar nature.

The subway was running, and Paris had a very elaborate subway. You could get most anywhere on it. I was coming back from somewhere one night and the car was very crowded, standing room only. Right next to me, so close that I was virtually squeezed between them, were a French girl and an American GI. She knew no English and he knew no French and yet they were doing pretty well by sign language and body language alone. He was obviously going home with her and they had some little difficulty about the arrangements. I offered my services as a French speaker and acted as inter-mediary making the arrangements for them, much to their delight as well as all the surrounding people. Everyone was crowded in so close that there must have been a half dozen people in on the situation and all enjoying it hugely. I got a big kiss for my reward and that was only one of many such experiences.

I took a lot of photographs that summer and did a lot of exploring. As part of our regular courses we did a lot of exploring among the ancient buildings of Paris. The Louvre had just reopened and we visited that of course. The Roman ruins were right in our neighborhood – the ruins of Roman baths which in the middle ages had been transformed into a monastery and which were now a museum. I was fascinated with the Roman brickwork, which was still intact and over the centuries had become rock hard. It was black in color and if you struck it with a hard object like a stone it would ring like metal. It had endured through a thousand years or so.

One of the most interesting experiences involved a piece of history in the making. That summer, Marshall Pétain – who had been the president of the French Vichy state under the Nazis – was tried by the French for treason. He was a very old man at that point. It was at the Palais de Justice and the courtroom was not very large. The audience was very restricted, mostly to officials, but Jack and I decided we would like very much to see this trial, if only briefly. We put on our best uniforms, got our identification papers and went down and presented ourselves to the guard at the door to the courtroom. He couldn't read any English. He looked at our papers, he looked at us, and we maintained a very grave demeanor. He admitted us, we went in and got up in the back of the balcony, standing room only. I guess we heard about fifteen minutes of the trial. It was all an argument by one of the counsel. Pretty soon one of the security men spotted us, probably having figured out that we weren't supposed to be there. He very quietly and politely stepped in close to us and asked us in a low voice who we were and what we were doing there. He then led us into the corridor and we explained the situation to him. He sort of laughed and told us he appreciated our interest, but we really weren't permitted to return. We left but we had had at least a fifteen-minute view of this bit of history.

Another interesting thing was at the Invalides, the building in which Napoleon's tomb rests in the rotunda. There's a huge courtyard and in that courtyard General DeGaulle was going to decorate the American colors and General Patton was going to decorate the French colors. It was a kind of exchange of compliments. Of all the military officers, those two were perhaps the biggest prima donnas, and to watch this ceremony was to see a demonstration of the most extreme possibilities of military formality. It was something to see. I think they tried to outperform each other. It was very impressively done.

My French language teacher was an older woman from Corsica, Madame Pandolfi. Earlier in life she had taught several years in a private school in Boston and she spoke English very well. She told me one day, "M. Richardson, you speak French with a marvelous New England accent." I took that to be an official compliment.

Our lodging was quite near the Luxembourg Gardens, which is a big park-like area around the Luxembourg Palace. The palace was partially blown up in a battle between the Germans and the French resistance. The Germans captured it and used it as a headquarters. The gardens were a beautiful park with sculpture, pools and a playground for the old people and the children of the area. We used to go over there and study from time to time. I believe the palace was later restored.

On one occasion we met Gertrude Stein, the American expatriate author. She was in the habit of walking her dog in Luxembourg Gardens close to where she lived and she was very interested in talking to American soldiers. When she saw us there, she would come and talk to us and ask questions like where we were from. One of the members of my group asked her why she had chosen to live in Paris all this time and in France even during the War. She said that whenever she was in the United States she never had a moment of privacy. She was chased by the press, people stopped her in the street, and it was a constant annoyance, but in Paris nobody paid any attention to her. She could go out and walk her dog and unless she took the initiative, no one bothered her at all. That was her explanation.

There was a very interesting 15th- or 16th-century church close to the University, St. Étienne du Mont, which had a fine organ in it that had been used for recordings, some of which were available in the U.S. I discovered, being an organ enthusiast, that the church organist practiced at about four in the afternoon for an hour or so, and I would slip in and sit in the back of the church. I also visited the church where César Franck had been organist all his life and had a chance to hear that organ.

These are just a few of the many things I was able to take advantage of during that summer in Paris. There were the erotic entertainments as well, a specialty of Paris, and we all went in for them and saw the full variety.

Those Paris days and nights were so full, with all kinds of sightseeing expeditions, studying, talking, and visiting the nightspots that were available in seemingly endless number. One that we visited was the famous nightclub, Le Bœuf Sur le Toit – literally the Bull on the Roof – famous from the twenties, the days of Hemingway and Fitzgerald and the expatriate Americans of that era. We went in and found a bar on the ground floor – the American bar. It was packed shoulder to shoulder with GIs. We went upstairs to the English bar. It was pretty well packed by English officers and they looked down their noses at ordinary American soldiers coming in. So we passed on that one and went to the third bar, which obviously was the gay bar. There was a smaller crowd there and they were very, very welcoming. We hadn't been there very long before one introduced himself to me as a count, a very courteous gentleman. He invited me to spend the weekend with him at his chateau outside Paris. I declined as courteously as he had invited, explaining that I had a very busy schedule. From the look in his eyes I had visions of Count Dracula and wondered whether I would escape if I went with him. In any case, I didn't go.

We hit the Folies Bergères once. That was a big show for tourists and after what we had seen of a more intimate nature, we weren't very excited by it. We did admire the vigor and enthusiasm that the performers demonstrated for that massive audience of GIs. As part of our studies we got to visit the Palace of Versailles and particularly admired the hall of mirrors where the Versailles treaty had been signed and the great gardens, part of which we found had been converted to vegetable gardens during the War.

However, of all the palaces I saw, the one that appealed to me most of all was Fontainebleau. A few miles from Paris, Fontainebleau represents virtually the whole history of France in architecture. I believe it was started around the 11th century and virtually every king of consequence added something to it, right up to the 19th century when Louis-Philippe added a wing. To a great extent the furnishings were still there. Napoleon's throne and Napoleon's camp bed – which would barely fit me – and Marie Antoinette's bedroom with its secret passage to a secret room, the purpose of which one could only imagine, were intact. There were many other rooms, including two large wings around the fore court which housed an art school, and I think still do.

The gardens had gone half wild during the War, which added a romantic touch to them. Also, in the town we had a French luncheon and for the first and last time I had rabbit, in the form of a rabbit casserole. I liked it from a culinary point of view, but it gave me a bad conscience. I'm fond of small animals of all kinds and the thought of eating a rabbit rather spoiled my enjoyment of the meal, but that was all that was on the menu.

The forest of Fontainebleau was an interesting place too. From an American point of view it's not a great forest, but its traditions with the painting school of Fontainebleau were familiar to us.

All of those things added to the excitement of that summer. Then, early in August, I was studying one sunny morning in the great court of the University. I was sitting by a large fountain and I heard a newsboy who had come into the court shouting "EXTRA" and waving his papers. He kept shouting something that I couldn't quite make out, so I motioned him to come to me. I bought his paper and what he had been shouting was, "La Bombe Atomique." The paper had huge headlines across the front filling the whole first page and describing the attack on a Japanese city by the atomic bomb.

That caused a great deal of interest among us because we anticipated with some dread that when we left Europe we'd get shipped to the Asian War, which none of us looked forward to. We all rejoiced that the atomic bomb was dropped on Japan and, all in all, I still think it was a good thing for the U. S. to have done. In the end I think it saved lives. The Japanese would have resisted invasion by massed forces of their troops, and they had access to both gas and germs, having used them in China. We would have attacked with every naval and air force that we had, and masses of soldiers. I am sure the loss of life would have been tremendous. Although the wounds from the atomic bomb, both immediate and long lasting, were terrible, I thought in the end it would have been even more terrible for both the U. S. and Japan had we had to do it by conventional means. I still think so.

Life in Paris in that summer of 1945 was unique. There was general chaos, through which small vistas of order opened and closed. What seemed possible one day was not possible the next. A package of cigarettes palmed at the right time and place could do magic. If you were an American GI, the possibilities were endless. It was an exhilarating time. Stability was to come with the autumn, but much of the magic would be lost.

XI

Occupation Duty

Going back to my outfit at the end of August, I found them encamped this time outside of the city of Ingolstadt in Bavaria on the Danube. Ingolstadt originated as a Roman city, and during the middle ages it was a great center of trade routes. It still holds both Roman ruins and medieval ruins and is presently a large and active city. I hadn't been there very long – about a month, I guess – and was supposedly doing occupation duty. But in reality not much of anything was going on and the men were being weeded out, sent in singles or twos or small groups to various outfits that were going to be in occupation long term. The men who had been in combat for some time, like me, high point men we were called, were going to be sent to outfits that were being made up to be sent home.

Before that happened I was able to get another three-day pass to Paris. So late in September I was back in Paris. This time things were different. For one thing the franc had been stabilized, the black market was more underground than it had been, and the season had changed, and that had a marked effect. It was rainy most of the time I was there. There was a certain melancholy hanging about the city on a rainy autumn evening. I did altogether enjoy the visit, however, but in a different mood from what I had been in during the summer. The mood among the other soldiers there seemed to be different too.

One thing I did, and was looking forward to strongly, was to pay another visit to the Palace of Fontainebleau. It was rainy, showery, but occasionally a little hazy sunshine showed through, and I spent a good deal of time around the gardens and in the palace itself just thinking of the centuries of autumns past and enjoying the quiet. There weren't many people there and it was very relaxing. It was in my mind a farewell to France.

Back in Bavaria I found myself alerted to move and was very shortly sent out to one of the units being made up of high-point men. This was a combat engineer unit, a free battalion, so called, since it was hitched directly to a corps and was more or less autonomous. It had been given occupation duty at the medieval walled city of Gunzburg, right on the Danube River not far west of Augsburg.

I settled my affairs with my old company. I said goodbye to the few that I still knew, Sarge and Jack, and off I went. I arrived together with a bunch of engineers from other units, truck drivers, bulldozer operators, crane operators, big husky men. And as we went through the line, I was the last one passing by the executive officer, who was checking each one of us out. He came to me, looked at me and said, "Soldier, you don't look like a truck driver." I said, "No sir, I am not a truck driver. I've never driven one." He said, "And I suppose you've never operated a backhoe, a bulldozer or a crane." "That's true. I never have," I replied. He said, "Well, somebody has fixed up your record. It says here you are an expert operator of all of these." Apparently somebody had wanted to qualify me for this unit. "What am I going to do with you?" he asked. I'd learned in the Army long before that when you have an opportunity of any sort you grab it and work out the details later.

I looked around and saw that it was an office setup. There were a couple of boys typing and doing paperwork. I turned to him and said, "Sir, I am an expert typist," which was true. He looked a little dubious, saying, "That's not on your records." I said, "Well, I learned long before I joined the Army." There was a typewriter unoccupied near there and he said, "All right, sit down and show me." I sat down and rapped out a bit on the typewriter. Then he read slowly from something he had there and had me type directly from his reading aloud. He said, "Well, I think we have a job for you. Our battalion records clerk is shipping out the end of this week. You stick with him while he's still here, learn his duties and you have a job." I did, and learning his duties was fairly easy. My record was fixed up to show me to be a clerk-typist. I was in.

It was a matter of taking the mail and all the bulletins that came in every day, sorting them out, directing them either to the executive officer or directly to the commanding officer and whatever. Soon I found I even had a private office, but I was the bottom man in the S1 section. The executive officer, the sergeant major and I were the S1 section. Before I got there, they had taken over what had been quite a nice office building, small, but nicely appointed, a modern building.

Our living quarters were in what had been a small tourist hotel. The name was Hotel zum Baren. The entire headquarters moved in there and took over the hotel. I roomed with the sergeant major of the battalion. We soon hit it off very well.

The hotel was run by a husband and wife who were delighted with this arrangement, because they apparently had not done too well under the Nazis. And now, their hotel filled with Americans, they were well paid. This was peacetime, after all, and they went out of their way to see that we were well fed and well taken care of.

The hotel was right next to a private forest that had been a hunting forest for the former kings of Bavaria. The Germans themselves were not permitted to hunt there, except under severe restrictions. We GIs were not governed by that, so we frequently augmented our diet by some of our crack shots going out into the forest and bringing back deer, something which I had nothing to do with, but I ate it.

One of the most interesting things among the bulletins that I got everyday was the report on black market operations that directly affected the military. I was astonished at what went on, mostly in Paris.

There were still large numbers of GIs AWOL there at the end of the War. One of the large scale operations was this. A driver of a gasoline truck, which was one of the big ten-wheelers loaded with five-gallon gasoline cans, would go through Paris en route to the front. He would make friends with a girl there. She would set it up with the black market and on his next trip through he would vanish along with truck, gasoline and all. He would sell the truck, the gasoline and everything and she would take him either to some quarter of Paris and hide him or out into the countryside with some of her relatives or friends and hide him out there.

Apparently this went on with some frequency, which meant considerable losses and considerable investigation. I suppose that would explain why the boy contact that I had in Paris had asked if I had a jeep or gasoline or tires for sale.

The most extreme example I saw was the disappearance of one of the Army engineers' steam locomotives on the railroad. It turned up later. It had been taken to a sidetrack somewhere in the Paris rail yards – which were extensive – dismantled completely, crated up, and shipped to Marseilles, which is on the Mediterranean coast. Half of it, before the investigators caught up with it, had already been shipped across to North Africa, I suppose to Tunisia or Algeria. The other half was crated up and waiting on the docks of Marseilles. The reports I got were reviewed and forwarded on to my commanding officer.

The men were doing simple occupation duty, which was pretty routine, and they were sweating out going home. This was only in the autumn, around October, and they were not to go home until the end of the winter. They were getting unruly to some degree, like stealing jeeps to go on joyrides. One of the things that had to be done was the preparation of summary courts martial, of which there were quite a few. This was the duty of the S1 office and it got passed down to me. I got quite adept at preparing the papers. This was my first introduction to the practice of law, which I later made my career. I soon got so good at it that they just automatically were sent to me to do. The cases ranged all the way from petty theft or fistfights to murder. There was one case in which an American soldier murdered a civilian Italian worker over the girl that they both pursued. That one went to higher echelons, but initially it had to be handled by our commanding officer.

I got to examine the rules that supposedly governed our headquarters and I found that a battalion such as ours was supposed to be equipped with certain military forms. There was quite a long list of them. Some of them seemed to me to be of doubtful or no use to us in our situation. I consulted the sergeant major. He consulted the executive officer and said, "Go ahead. Order them." I prepared the order, sent it off to Paris and forgot it.

A couple of weeks later a two-and-a-half-ton truck arrived from Paris loaded with forms. Fortunately, each form had its own carton, but there was a tremendous stack of them and I said, "What am I going to do with these?" And everybody else did too. The solution was to put my boys to work. These were three German boys, still in their teens, who had deserted the German army at the end of the War over on the Russian front. They managed to escape through Germany westward and ended up there in Bavaria. They were very useful. They were willing to do anything and they had no place to stay, so I was put in charge of them. I put them in our cellar where there was a very comfortable storage room next to the furnace room. They were to keep the furnace running and do the janitorial jobs, in exchange for which they could fix up the room to live in. We fed them regular rations and provided what they needed. Under my direction they put shelves up all around my office to house those forms. Among the forms was a discharge from the Army, which couldn't be used in Europe anyway, but some of the men came in just to look at it and hope. Life went on that way.

I had quite a bit of spare time during this period. In the days before I got into the Army I used to do a good deal of pen sketching, having learned that technique by copying the illustrations to *Alice in Wonderland* by that great English illustrator, Tenniel. I put up a number of fantasy drawings, frogs under toadstools, and things of that nature, on the wall just here and there where there were openings in the shelves or on the shelves. One day we got a surprise inspection from higher echelons. They went around the whole place and finally they hit my office. Everyone stood around this colonel who came in. My commanding officer, the executive officer, the sergeant major and two of the other officers were all there. Everyone awaited comments from the colonel. He looked around. "Very good, very good. Got more forms than any other office in the ETO." He said. "That's good. That's good." Then he saw my little sketches and he looked at them and said, "Who did these?" I said, "I did sir." Everyone was sort of hanging silent waiting to see what his reaction would be. I was wondering whether I was going to be court martialed or sent to the latrines or what. He thought about it a moment, then he turned to the commanding officer and said, "That's good. That's good. You should encourage your soldiers under these circumstances, to pursue any little hobbies they have. That will keep them interested. We're having too many disorders, too many courts martial out here." And off he went. I was the fair-haired boy after that and everything went fine.

I've already mentioned that the teenagers were among those who recovered first from the shock of war among the civilians. We made an arrangement through a teenage boy – he was probably about fifteen – that his mother and sister would do laundry for the sergeant major and me and some of the other members of the headquarters. We thought it was maybe time for us to spruce up a bit. The War was over and we ought to look more like proper soldiers. They did a good job and this boy was assigned to mediate. We paid him with cigarettes. The sergeant major was a heavy smoker and in our bedroom there was always an ashtray filled with butts. He was one of those smokers who would smoke just a little bit of a cigarette and then stamp it out. So the butts were big ones. The boy noticed these and he asked if he could take those butts also, and we said, "Sure, take them." I noticed he had two separate containers for them. One for the new cigarettes he was taking in payment, a nice little cigarette case, and the other one a cardboard box into which he'd put the butts. I said to him one day, "I noticed that you separate these. Why do you want the both of them like this?" He said, giving me a grin, "You know, the butts I give to my mother and sister. They think that's what I am getting for payment and I keep the new cigarettes to myself." I thought to myself, here is one of future Germany's entrepreneurs. He was really making out because cigarettes were the coin of the realm.

Among other things that he could produce were silver five-mark pieces from the old days in Germany, before the Nazi era. These pieces were a little bigger than the old American silver dollar and they had a very high silver content. Local silversmiths, we had discovered, could make them into very credible rugged-looking men's rings. A lot of the Germans had apparently saved up these coins. They were useless in the Nazi era, but they'd saved them up hoping that someday they'd be valuable. Because they were high in silver they were valuable for that alone. He produced many of these for us. He could produce other things, too, in the way of souvenirs like

Nazi material. At the end of the War, people hid them away or destroyed them, but American soldiers loved anything with the Nazi insignia as souvenirs. When this was realized, people began digging them out and selling them for cigarettes to the soldiers. Our boy could produce a number of these. I don't know where he got a lot of this stuff. He probably had been a member of the Hitler Jugend, but that was in the past and he was a personable boy, and an obviously enterprising one.

The Bavarians had been hit less hard by the War than those in north and central Germany and they were quite friendly to us – all of them – not only the young ones, but the older ones were also less hostile. I noticed something about the German civilian population. Once they had accepted that the War was over, for them it was indeed over. Even former soldiers, at least on the face of it, were quite peaceable. We had no trouble at all from any of them, civilians or ex-soldiers. When they came in to surrender at the end of the War, soldiers did it with apparent willingness – even eagerness – to surrender to us rather than to the Russians. It was only the real hard line Nazis, the ones who had reason to be afraid of prosecution and imprisonment, who remained hostile.

The Hotel zum Baren provided us with music with our principal meal of the day in the form of a Polish band. These Poles had been slave workers. Now freed, they didn't want to go back to Poland. The Russians dominated the part of Poland they had come from and that country was still too turbulent so they made up a band. There was only one problem. All they could play were polkas. Some polkas are all right, but an endless concert of polkas day after day gets a little bit monotonous. Some of the American boys tried to teach them some

Blood and Candles

The Battalion kitchen crew, including several Poles who traded kitchen work for food. Many Poles, who had been forced to work for the Nazis, preferred to remain in the part of Germany controlled by the Allies rather than to return to their homeland under the Russians.

Occupation Duty

American music. They managed to learn some of the American popular songs, but somehow they all came out as polkas. They couldn't get away from that polka beat. It was a sort of standing joke. A new song would appear on the scene and then someone would say, "Well, let's see if our boys will polka-ize this one." And they did.

Christmas that year was very cheerful. Our regular supplies of food included turkeys and the boys brought in a deer. We shared those things with the German staff and a merry Christmas was had by all.

Winter there in Gunzburg was not very severe. It's hops country. By February, signs of spring were beginning to appear. We were cheered when the word came down early in February that, "You're going home." All the preparations were made. It was a mad time getting everything packed up and stored. Then the day came and we were trucked all the way to northern Germany, to Bremerhaven on the Baltic coast. We spent some time there in Bremerhaven waiting for the ship that was going to take us and it stormed all the time. The climate there was terrible, cold, windy, rain, freezing rain and sleet and generally messy. However, we used a German army barracks that was first rate. It had showers and all the equipment necessary to care for a large number of men.

XII

Heading Home

Finally, the ship was ready. It was a victory ship, four hundred feet long. We crowded in. A black quartermasters unit was also in the front section and we were packed in pretty well. We headed out. The same day a storm set in. We were going out into the North Sea, then the English channel and from there into the Atlantic. For four days that ship labored and plunged through terrific seas and gale winds. We were stacked six high in bunks. I had the good fortune to get a top bunk right under a vent screen, so I was getting plenty of fresh air. Nevertheless, I was seasick for the first time in my life, really seasick, terribly sick but only for a few hours. Some of the men were so sick that they had to be hospitalized in the infirmary and rendered unconscious. Some were sick for days.

I recovered after the first day and once I could get out on deck – which wasn't until we got out into the Atlantic and out of the storm – I enjoyed it. The effect was terrible on those black men in the bow section, because the ship would rear up on the waves and when the waves had gone under it, it would come down with a tremendous crash, the bow hitting as if it were hitting solid stone. I was afraid for a while the thing would disintegrate. But it didn't, and we survived. The piano in the rec room did not, however – it broke loose, struck a wall and exploded with one tremendous chord.

Heading Home

We got out into the Atlantic and although it was fairly rough going – this was in late February after all – it was bearable. I made friends with the ship's cat. He was a beat-up-looking old tomcat and he had a place outside when the weather was satisfactory, right under the galley vent, which meant that he got a warm draft of air and could smell what was being cooked in the galley. That was one smart cat. One of the cooks told me that when they docked, the cat would go ashore and he'd have his shore leave just like the crew, but he always got back to the ship in time. He and I became real buddies on the way over. I'd slip him a little goodie now and then.

We saw no other ships to speak of until we got near the United States. I don't remember now how long it took us, but it was a lot longer coming home than the *Île de France* took going over in spite of the *Île de France* having to go on the long detour to avoid German submarines. We arrived back in New York early one morning. I remember sighting the Statue of Liberty and oh, what a pleasant sight that was, a welcome sight. We made it into port.

Things happened so fast and with such complexity thereafter I really don't remember much about them, except that a sort of release document had to be executed for each one of us and the officer in command was so drunk that he wasn't able to do it. He said, "Richie, sign these damned things for me." So I sat down and spent about two hours one night signing his name to all of them, including the one for myself.

There remained only the formal discharge, which took place without ceremony. This was 1946, already early March. I got the train back to Maine. As I watched the stone walls go by and that early spring New England landscape, although there was no real sign of spring as yet, a great feeling of relaxation came over me, a kind of solidifying feeling. At last I knew it was all over and I was going home.

Postscript

I'm finishing the last tape on the 26th day of November in the year 2000. I'm approaching my 80th year and I have recalled all these things with the benefit of my photo album, and also some maps of Germany. My speaking here has been largely spontaneous as the things come to me, as if I were dictating a letter to a friend.

For a period of three months after returning home I was on a high from getting released and then plunged into a depression for about another three months, worked out of that, and thereafter went on with my life and left the War behind me. For many years after the War, I never thought much about it, although for eight years I suffered war nightmares with decreasing frequency. After that eight-year period I never had one again.

In recent years, since about the time of the celebration of the 50th anniversary of the end of the War, I've been more and more visited by these memories and dictating them to a tape brought a great feeling of release for me.

I hope whoever listens to the tapes or reads this transcription enjoys my story too, and can get a little picture of what it was like in those days to be part of the wartime life as a common soldier. I would never want to go through any such thing again. On the other hand, I feel it was an incomparable experience to have participated in the greatest events of my generation.

About the Author

Edward T. Richardson, Jr. was born in Portland, Maine on August 22, 1921. His family moved to South Portland in 1925, where he has lived since that time. He is a graduate of South Portland High School and Bowdoin College. He took courses at the University of Paris while serving with the Army in 1945 and after the War he attended Northeastern University Law School on the GI Bill, graduating in 1950.

His activities as a member of the United States Army in the Second World War, including extensive combat experience, are documented in this book. He received the Combat Infantry Badge for the European Theater and North Atlantic Theater of Operations ribbons.

Mr. Richardson was admitted to the Maine Bar in 1950 and became associated with a law firm specializing in insurance company defense work. His law practice soon branched out into a variety of fields including real estate and probate law and a specialization in conservation law.

In addition to his law practice Mr. Richardson also operated an insurance photography business, taught Constitutional Law at the Portland University Law School, and was a Field Investigator for the American Bar Foundation in connection with legal representation for indigent defendants in the Maine criminal courts. He has served on both state and local boards and commissions relating to the environment.

About the Author

As a lawyer Mr. Richardson is most noted for his pioneering work in the formation and development of several conservation organizations, most notably The Nature Conservancy, to which he devoted thirty years as counsel, trustee and officer. He wrote Maine's first Conservation Easement statute, was a founding member and secretary of the organization that pushed through the referendum that resulted in the acquisition of the Bigelow Mountain Range as a public domain, and he is the author of a history of the Maine chapter of The Nature Conservancy published in 1989.

In 1983 he received the Sol Feinstone Environmental Award, a cash award administered by the State University of New York, in recognition of his contributions to conservation of the natural environment.

Since his high school years Mr. Richardson has been an avid photographer and some of his wartime photographs are included in this book. He has taught and lectured in the field of nature photography and has made a particular specialty of black and white photography, developing and printing his own work since 1935. His photographs have been exhibited and published from time to time and he has received numerous awards for his photographic work.

Memberships include the Josselyn Botanical Society, the Maine Mycological Society, the Sigma Nu Fraternity, serving as Secretary of the House Corporation of the Iota Nu Chapter at the University of Southern Maine for more than 20 years, the Cumberland County Bar Association, the Veterans of Foreign Wars, the Photographic Historical Society of New England, the Portland Camera Club, serving as President,

Secretary, Treasurer and Trustee at various times, the Leica Historical Society, the Portland Society of Art, the Maine Historical Society, the Portland Senior Lawyers Association, and the Appalachian Mountain Club.

In 1995 Mr. Richardson participated in The Permanence of Memory: Maine Veterans and Civilians Remember World War II project.

His interests and hobbies over the years, in addition to photography, have included hiking, camping and mountain climbing. Throughout his life he has had a passionate interest in classical music and he has a substantial record collection.

A Note about the Type

Blood and Candles is composed in Dante, a type originally created for fine letterpress-printed book editions. Dante is classified as an old-style type, but it has somewhat darker "color" than many old-styles, and a particularly pleasing italic. Dante was developed by Italian master printer Giovanni (Hans) Mardersteig and French punch-cutter Charles Malin, for use as a private type in Mardersteig's own book-printing projects. The type first appeared in Mardersteig's 1955 edition of Boccaccio's *Trattatello in laude di Dante*. Once it was made available as a commercial font through the English Monotype Company, Dante was eagerly adopted by book designers and printers everywhere.

The book's display type is **Albertus**, drawn for Monotype by the noted goldsmith, lettering artist, typographer, teacher and printing historian Berthold Wolpe. Wolpe based Albertus on the letter forms he had been cutting by hand in bronze, and much of this liveliness remains in the typeface.

OWEN COUNTY PUBLIC LIBRARY

LaVergne, TN USA
25 January 2011
213966LV00002B/38/A

9 781553 692973